# Woody Allen

An illustrated biography by MYLES PALMER

**PROTEUS**

London and New York

PROTEUS BOOKS is an imprint of
The Proteus Publishing Group

*United Kingdom*
PROTEUS (PUBLISHING) LIMITED
Bremar House,
Sale Place,
London, W2 1PT.

*United States*
PROTEUS PUBLISHING COMPANY

*distributed by*
CHARLES SCRIBNER'S SONS
597 Fifth Avenue,
New York, N.Y. 10017

ISBN 0 906071 39 9 (Limp edition)
ISBN 0 906071 41 0 (Casebound edition)
First published in U.K. October 1980
First published in U.S. December 1980
© 1980 by Myles Palmer and
Proteus Publishing Company.
All rights reserved.

Typeset, printed and bound in Italy
by International Publishing Enterprises, Rome

# Contents

# Source Acknowledgements

The following sources have been consulted in researching this book:

*When the Shooting Stops... the Cutting Begins,* a very entertaining memoir by film editor Ralph Rosenblum;
*Crazy Like A Fox,* by S.J. Perelman;
*Getting Even,* by Woody Allen;
Film '78 (TV Special);
Time magazine;
A Golden Hour of Woody Allen (record album);
Chicago Tribune;
The New Yorker;
Time Out magazine;
New Musical Express;
London Evening Standard;
New York Times;
Village Voice;
Vogue magazine;
The Observer;
Sight and Sound;
National Lampoon.

# Preface

Scene: at seven each morning, America's comic conscience gets out of bed in his penthouse high above Fifth Avenue, overlooking the lakes and trees of Central Park. He puts on the same clothes he wore in *Annie Hall,* writes all day, then goes out for a late dinner at Elaine's with such pals as collaborator Marshall Brickman, actor Michael Murphy and *Saturday Night Live* producer Jean Doumanian. He comes home. From his terrace, where he filmed many of the cityscapes for the opening montage of his masterpiece, he looks out over Manhattan.

New York is his town, and it always will be.

# Introduction

Woody Allen is unique.

He was a joke-writer in the Fifties, a comedian in the Sixties, and a film director in the Seventies. When he started in movies he knew how to be funny but he did not know how to make films, which was a handicap. When it comes to doing something as technically complex and expensive as making a film, it helps to have experience or, at least, training. Clint Eastwood had seven years on *Rawhide* to see how horse operas were put together. Polanski studied for four years at a film school in Poland which was the best in the world at that time. Shooting feature films is the most expensive entertainment ever devised, and when such astronomical sums of money are being spent, it helps to know what you are doing. As Orson Welles once commented, it's the biggest train set in the world.

At first it was a case of taking the camera and running around Puerto Rico and Hungary, and learning by trial and error. His early films were creatively chaotic. They were gags and sketches and monologues, with bodies attached to the jokes. *Bananas* was essentially a one-character movie, as was *Sleeper,* while *Annie Hall* was a duet. The sophisticated *Manhattan* showed several characters interacting amusingly and effectively in a stylish, disciplined comedy classic.

Today his plots are better shaped, his directing style is fluent and personal, his acting is exceptionally subtle and his scintillating wit is as sharp as ever.

In the last eleven years his artistic growth has been phenomenal. He has earned his success. Woody Allen is a little man who has not gotten taller, but he has gotten bigger.

# The nice New Yorker

At a time when wits claim that being a New Yorker is never having to say you're sorry, Woody Allen is more apologetic than anyone, a man who has always said his one regret in life is that he is not someone else. Allen Stewart Konigsberg was born in Brooklyn on December 1st, 1935. His father was variously a waiter, a cab-driver and a jewelry engraver and his mother was a bookkeeper in a Manhattan florist shop. In high school he began writing gags and selling them to a PR company who would have them placed in gossip columns, attributed to their star clients. He changed his name. Instead of sounding like a lager, he sounded like an American. In 1968 when Woody's path crossed with that of film editor Ralph Rosenblum, the two men found that they had a lot in common. In his book *When The Shooting Stops... The Cutting Begins* (Viking Press), Rosenblum, born in 1925, gives a sobering account of the Brooklyn Jewish community where he spent the first twenty years of his life:

> Bensonhurst was tidier, stabler and more genteel than the commotion-prone Lower East side where the newcomers thronged, but its lessons and ways were those of impoverished immigrants hanging on desperately to the niche they had made for themselves. Thrift, self-improvement and a thudding practicality ruled

everything, a heavy-spirited regime that was molded into perma-nence by the weight of the Depression. Ten years later when Woody Allen was growing up in the same milieu, its values and oppressive conformity would still prevail.

When Woody first became a professional funnyman the traditions and technologies of entertainment had reached an interesting stage. Screen comedy had been created in the Twenties and Thirties by Chaplin, Buster Keaton, Harold Lloyd and Harry Langdon, who kept audiences laughing till the talkies came along. In the Thirties some of the stars of the vaudeville stage and Broadway made it in films, performers such as W.C. Fields, Jimmy Durante and Eddie Cantor. Later the traditions of vaudeville con-tinued into television. Early TV was more or less video vaudeville, and comedians like Jackie Gleason, Sid Caesar and Milton Berle became the superstars of the new medium in the Fifties.

In those days, TV was live. Performers were not protected by technology as they are now. Each 60 or 90-minute show was a comedy-revue which lived or died from moment to moment in front of a live audience and was

*A private tennis game.*

broadcast as it happened. The king of these sudden death spectaculars, a man worshipped and respected by other comedians, was Sid Caesar. Sid's humor was more sophisticated and satirical than his chief rivals. One of the legends of American showbiz, he is virtually unknown outside the United States, for reasons we shall see in a moment.

Still in his twenties when *Your Show of Shows* started in 1950, handsome Sid was a dynamo, and a big dynamo, over six feet tall. Mel Brooks once said of him: "He could kill a Buick with his bare hands — punch it in the grille and kill it." Sid's success was immense. *Your Show of Shows* ran for four seasons, after which he did three years of *Caesar's Hour.* Among many gifted writers on the *Your Show Of Shows* team were Mel Brooks, Lucille Kallen, Mel Tolkin and, for a time, Neil Simon and his brother Danny. Those who worked on *Caesar's Hour* included Carl Reiner (who later directed *Where's Poppa,* and more recently *The Jerk*), Larry Gelbart (who created *M\*A\*S\*H*) and the precocious Woody Allen who joined this team when he was about 25.

After a final series of *Sid Caesar Invites You* in 1959 the man widely regarded as the finest comedian in TV history vanished from the tube. Overnight, a giant had disappeared, forced into premature semi-retirement, secluded in his mansion-fortress in Beverley Hills. Ten years is a lifetime in TV, though, and while the meteoric Sid burned brightly across a decade, he owed a lot of his glory to the format and to his back-up team. Having rocketed to stardom so quickly, before he had served an apprenticeship which might have taught him to sing, dance and act, he found himself lacking the versatility of others who were geared for longer careers.

This was perhaps a salutary lesson to Woody who had seen the mighty Sid go onstage in front of a theater-sized audience every week knowing that any mistake he made would be seen coast-to-coast. A man who was a hero every week for ten years was now suddenly obsolete. Maybe it was then that Woody became aware of the need for long-term career planning for an active middle age.

As it worked out for him, he was able to use his skill as a writer to become a comedian himself, and use his success as a comedian to get work writing films, and eventually to direct films himself.

Ace film critic Pauline Kael has usually been pretty much pro-Allen. She rightly emphasizes how polite and mild-mannered he is.

> Woody Allen appears before us as the battered adolescent, scarred forever, a little too nice and much too threatened to allow himself to be aggressive. He has the city-wise effrontery of a shrimp who began by using language to protect himself and then discovered that language has a life of its own. The running war between the tame and the surreal — between Woody Allen the frightened nice guy trying to keep the peace and Woody Allen the wiseacre whose subversive fantasies keep jumping out of his mouth — has been the source of the comedy in his films.

> He has found a nonaggressive way of dealing with urban pressures. He stays nice; he's not insulting, like most New York comedians, and he delivers his zingers without turning into a cynic. We enjoy his show of defenselessness, and even the I-don't-mean-any-harm ploy, because we see the essential sanity in him. We respect that sanity — it's the base from which he takes flight.

Other Jewish boys from Brooklyn have not been so sane. Norman Mailer turned out to be a hoodlum genius whose reputation for bad taste and public misbehavior spanned three decades. As two-fisted Norm boozed, and boasted his way through orgies of inflated prose, ever threatening to climax in one gigantic explosion of self-hype and bad karma, we sometimes wondered whether any country but America could have produced him, or indeed whether any country but the USA would have tolerated him.

Today Woody's recent films do big business in big cities because in what they describe, dramatize and satirize they are totally urban. Cities are endlessly interesting and entertaining and in the Ultimate City, from Runyon on Broadway to Scorcese on Little Italy to Woody on pseudo-intellectual Manhattan, there's raw material aplenty.

By comparison, life in Los Angeles, where you can rely on about 340 days of sun a year, and where there are 40 miles of beach, sometimes seems to be better suited as a subject for rock music than films. Peaceful easy feelings, life in the fast lane, and all that. Some streets, like Wilshire Boulevard, are 20 miles long! Heaven is the sun, motor motion and the next sexual encounter. Lifestyles are pleasant, random, transient, and, finally, dull. Whereas New York is stimulating, a city of issues, challenges and subcultures, of fringes, streetlife and undergrounds. And clubs. There are jazz clubs and folk clubs and New Wave clubs and rock discos and off-off-Broadway theaters, and galleries, and plenty of things happening to write stories and plays about. Scenes, lofts, studios and experiments proliferate and cross-fertilize.

In LA, there is no underground. All the action revolves round big names and big deals. It is almost impossible to be discovered there. You don't go to LA to make it. Rather, when you've made it, you go to LA to Really Make It.

Another Jewish-Manhattan comedy genius is Neil Simon, who went to live in California with actress Marsha Mason, after the tragic death of his wife Joan. The king of comedy playwrights was obliged to abandon his milieu in order to escape from the ghosts of his past, and start a new life with his second wife. Simon was interviewed in *Playboy* after he had been away from New York for three years, and said he could never be a Californian if he lived there another 50 years, although he could see the virtues of both environments. "There's a *lot* that I like about California but I miss the vibrations and the almost electrical input you get from New York City."

Simon's views were typically succinct and witty. "For instance, in New York I like to walk down the street and meet people and say 'How are you? What are you doing tomorrow night?' But you don't bump into *anyone* in Los Angeles. And if you do they are invariably involved in show business, and they talk about the business all the time. Another thing: In California, everybody's got these plastic smiles and they always want to make life pleasant. They've taken the *conflict* out of it. I think that in Southern California, people are very concerned about making their life comfortable, while back East they're more concerned with making their life interesting. If I had to make one comparison, I'd say that when it's five below in New York, it's 78 in Los Angeles, and when it's 110 in New York, it's 78 in Los Angeles: but there are two million interesting people in New York — and only 78 in Los Angeles. There may be a hell of a lot more, but it's hard to find them. Everybody in Los Angeles wants to be a movie director. That's all you hear: 'Well, I really want to *direct.*' "

Many of the more creative elements in American entertainment feel the same way. Al Pacino still lives in the same comparatively humble bohemian apartment he has lived in for years. Of LA, director Paul Mazursky has said: "It is a company town and you cannot stop talking about film. It is also a lotus land — not that a bit of lotus does any harm to anyone from time to time. The real regeneration, though, comes down here in the Village, where there's humanity, there's theater and there are books."

Even early in his career, the lotus held no magnetic attraction for Woody Allen, who always knew who he was, where he was, what he was, and where he wanted to stay. He was aware that Malibu massages, while Manhattan energizes. California, he always felt, was somewhere he should strive to avoid. "When I was young" he told *Time,* "I was always very careful not to get seduced into TV writing. I was making a lot of money and knew it was a dead end; you get seduced into a lifestyle, move to California, and in six months you become a producer!"

Woody broadly agrees with Neil Simon. "I like cities," he says, "and I've seen some in my life. But of all the cities I've been to, I like New York the best. Because it's simply very exciting, active. Paris has that kind of feeling, too. I could live there very happily. I don't like the city of Los Angeles because it just isn't a city. I have lived in London for about eight months, years ago, and I like it very much, but I prefer Paris. What I feel about New York is hard to say in a few words. It's really the rhythm of the city. You feel it the moment you walk down the street. There's hundreds of good restaurants, thousands of brilliant paintings, you can see all the old movies, all the new ones — and still that's not what makes it different from other cities. "It's an intangible rhythm that's there. Paris has it, London doesn't. It has to do with nerves, with the blood that runs through the city. It's dangerous, noisy. It's not peaceful or easy and because of it you feel more alive. It's more in keeping with what human beings are meant to feel about the world. In a way its more Darwinian. There's more conflict than anywhere else. The struggle to survive here is much more exciting than Los Angeles, say, where everything is pleasant. I mean, all those people sitting in their tubs, can you imagine it?"

Woody is very complimentary about British comedians. In a Film 78 Special he told producer Iain Johnstone that he had been an aficionado of English humor for a long time. "I've always been crazy about those films of the Fifties and maybe into the Sixties. All those wonderful Peter Sellers and Alec Guinness movies, they were sensational. I'm a big, big English comic fan. Alistair Sim, the *Beyond The Fringe* players. They always make me laugh, to this day. Whenever I see Cook in New York, I always find him hilarious. I always watch Monty Python when I have a chance to."

He has also been extra-nice to his associates. Editor Rosenblum says he has advanced the careers of many associates, and is very generous with the people he values. "Ex-wives and girl friends star in his films, and actors with walk on parts get title credits. My lead credits in *Annie Hall* and *Interiors* are, to my knowledge, the only instances in which an editor has been so honored."

Last year The New Yorker cinema, at Broadway and 88th St., had a director's season which was advertized as The Woody Allen New Yorker Film Festival. Nine of his films were showing and fans could see up to six of them in one day, plus *Manhattan* which was on general release. Ten films showing in your own hometown! Did he still wish he was someone else? Probably. At least Fassbinder never gets pestered by strangers in the street who think he is a cuddly bundle of fun, or hears his name constantly shouted from passing cars and trucks.

# Standing up for himself

Woody on being kidnaped as a child:

> I got into the car with them. They drive me off and they send a ransom note to my parents. And my father has bad reading habits. He gets into bed at night with the ransom note and he read half of it and he got drowsy and fell asleep... then he lent it out. Meanwhile, they take me to New Jersey, bound and gagged, and my parents finally realized that I'm kidnaped and they snap into action immediately. They rent out my room. The ransom note says for my father to leave $1000 in a hollow tree in New Jersey. He has no trouble raising a $1000, but he gets a hernia carrying the hollow tree.

The job of stand-up comedian is one of the scariest jobs in the world. If you are a musician you can hide behind loud drums and electric guitars, and even a boxer can hide for part of the time by feinting, holding and back-pedaling. And remember, there are three men in the ring. The referee is there to stop the fight before you get killed.

But a comedian goes out alone, with nowhere to hide. He needs to appear cool and confident. However well-rehearsed he is, and however many good jokes he has, he knows that at any moment a mispronounced word or a wrong pause or hand movement can distract the audience and kill the laugh. So he stands there and makes fun of his private life, or imaginary, exaggerated aspects of his private life, and he mocks the fads and foibles of the age he lives in. He knows where the laughs are, or should be, and every time they don't laugh he dies, and on a bad night he dies a thousand deaths. He wishes he had never been born.

He is vulnerable. Even the finest comedians are constantly aware of their vulnerability and never more so than at the beginning of their act. At the start of one of his live albums Richard Pryor says "I hope I'm funny!" which summarizes his feelings with perfect candor and perfect brevity. You can talk about nerves and panic and stage fright till you are green in the face, but the fear comes down to those four simple words: "I hope I'm funny!"

Among strictly verbal comedians Mort Sahl is one of those Woody most admires. "Sahl is a genius," he says. "He's like Charlie Parker was in jazz, he has such energy and such technique and such conviction that if you're in the same room as him you can't think about anything else."

The careers of many comedians are often short, even tragic. People told Lenny Bruce he was ahead of his time, and, ultra-frustrated, he became a junkie and killed himself. Kamikaze, a martyr. Others with less self-destructive impulses moved out of the clubs into TV, the land of the bland and the big bucks.

Television is merciless and all-consuming, and particularly cruel to comedians. You can sing the same song on ten different shows but you can't tell the same joke. TV consumes comedians because it consumes their best material. The trick is to use it, and not let it use you. Or, alternately, to stop being a comedy star and become a TV star instead, which was the fate of a few smart, lucky entertainers from the Fifties who became chat show hosts.

It's interesting to note that British and American chat shows differ in the backgrounds of their anchormen. In the UK, guys like Michael Parkinson and Russell Harty are journalists, whereas in the USA the moguls of tele-talk have usually been ex-comedians like Dick Cavett, Merv Griffin and the king of them all, Johnny Carson. For many years Carson has started his five-nights-a-week show with a comedy monologue, but he is really an intermediary, an interpreter, a linkman who shares the spotlight and presides over a series of guests who come on to plug their latest film, show, album or book.

The role requires a degree of curiosity and generosity which, if not real, must appear real. The host must be a versatile actor who can dispense frivolous junk with exactly the right amount of grace and throwaway

*The young stand-up comedian keeps it under his hat.*

charm. It is nowhere near as easy as Carson makes it look. Obviously if Woody had become a talk show host he would never have had the super-success which Carson had simply because he looks like a completely different animal.

Carson is confidence, Allen is anxiety. With his sporty good looks, Johnny Carson personifies a type, the amusingly casual young middle-aged man, a silver-tongued, silver-haired devil-may-care winner. He has an aura of dynamism, even athleticism. Next to him Woody Allen looks like a nervy, edgy little assistant librarian. Johnny looks like a well-adjusted winner who enjoys life, and Woody looks like a mal-adjusted misfit who gets ignored, ridiculed and molested. Still, enough of the empty speculation about what Woody might have done as a chatterbox-interviewer. What was he like as a comedian in the mid-Sixties?

Placing one of his albums on the turntable in the 1980s, you do not know what to expect. In the LP sleeve photo he looks very young, and the picture is cropped in such a way as to make him look alarmingly like Elvis Costello, himself a bespectacled *enfant terrible* of another era.

The record is on the Golden Hour label and is titled Golden Hour Presents Woody Allen. You suspect it might be tame, feeble and dated. It may have been funny in 1964, you believe, or boring, or half-funny, or occasionally funny, but whatever it was then it will not be funny sixteen years later. How wrong can you be?

The album is brilliant. It is crammed with dynamite material and reveals Woody as a master of the spoken word, with hardly a redundant line or a flabby phrase anywhere. It is full of wildly funny routines and anecdotes. His chatter is exceptionally witty and the high points of the comedy are very high indeed. He is consistently clever and inventive, he has a comic personality as powerful and appealing as an Ernie Bilko, and in terms of sheer joke-writing he compares favorably with the best scripts of all-time classic TV shows like *Monty Python.*

Of course, some of the gags have dated, and a few references may be a little esoteric for some people. For instance he recalls how he has fun with a swinging blonde who had BIRD LIVES! tattooed on the inside of her thigh. Unless you know something of the life and legend of jazz genius Charlie Parker, this line means nothing. Parker was an alto sax player of phenomenal virtuosity, perhaps the greatest soloist in the history of jazz. Such was his quicksilver inspiration that his music seemed to swoop and dart and fly, and he was nicknamed Yardbird, or Bird. A legendary figure, he was worshipped with almost religious intensity and when he died, a heroin addict, at the age of 34, grafitti immediately appeared on the walls of the subways in New York: BIRD LIVES! Not everyone knows all this, though, so the gag is somewhat elitist.

Come to think of it, this may not have been one of Allen's fantastic imaginings. Maybe a few female jazzniks really did have such messages branded on their skin. Jazz fans have been known to be guilty of the occasional eccentricity!

Generally, Woody's subject matter on the album is accessible. It ranges over the same areas he was later to feature in his films: Jewish family life, college, psychoanalysis, mugging, love, sex, marriage and divorce. He delights in telling how he came from a tough neighborhood where it was hard being the sensitive one going to violin lessons when the other kids were stealing hub-caps from moving cars. Mostly it's underdog humor, a style Woody has since made his own. He tells how Dad was a caddie at a miniature golf course, how his parents had no money, watched the Ed Sullivan show and rooted their values in "God — and carpeting". His boyhood adventures are mainly concerned with being beaten up and abused by assorted schoolmates and thugs.

At this stage of his career Allen was a cult, a contender, a smart young man with a fast mouth and a keen wit which skated cleverly round their subjects, skilfully touching many bases. He can fling together a few fragments about Jewishness and death, and throw them away in a couple of deceptively biting lines. Brandishing a gold pocketwatch proudly, he comments:

> My grandfather on his deathbed sold me this watch. My grandfather was a very insignificant man. At his funeral the hearse followed the other cars.

His preoccupations mirror the preoccupations of young adults at the time. City life and college life allow him to show off the academic and intellectual sides of his humor. He scorns phoney sophistication and pretence. With a few rapier-thrusts he can sketch and demolish the pretentious circles where arty Bohemian girls wear black make-up and leotards and have their ears pierced with conductor's punches. And sit around listening to record albums by Marcel Marceau!

> I went to NYU myself. I was a philo major there. I took all the abstract philosophy courses in college like Truth and Beauty, Advanced Truth and Beauty, Intermediate Truth, Introduction to God and Death 101.
> I was thrown out of NYU in my freshman year. I cheated on my Metaphysics Final. I looked within the soul of the boy sitting next to me!
> I was in love in my freshman year, but I didn't marry the first girl I fell in love with... 'cos there was a tremendous religious conflict at the time. She was an atheist and I was an agnostic. We didn't know what religion *not* to bring the children up in.

In the last twenty years dope has become a huge industry in the USA, a culture-within-a-culture. And since drugs have become such a prominent feature of American life, Woody's line on the subject has hardened. He does not approve. In fact, his anti-dope stand is one of the most persistent and easily-identifiable themes in his work. Let *Cheech and Chong* and *High Times* and *Rolling Stone* celebrate dope culture, he says, but I think

23

it's gone beyond a joke.

However, back in '64 dope seemed to be just another fad, another contemporary foible, another passing craze like hula-hoops and Davy Crockett hats. No one could foresee that the hippie Love Generation would turn the distribution and sale of illegal drugs into a gigantic billion dollar netherworld business.

When Woody first started working in clubs he sometimes met people he used to know when he was younger. He recalls bumping into a schooldays acquaintance who has turned, surprisingly, from the Boy Most Likely to Succeed into a wizened junkie. "He's living in the Village with a girl I used to know from Business Administration who is a junkette. They're gonna get married and I wanted to give them a wedding present. I didn't know what to get the junkie who has everything and I thought maybe a 16-piece starter set of silverware would be nice — all spoons!" Nowadays Woody simply would not descend as far as making a flip gag about hard drugs. Smack kills. Heroin is not funny.

First and foremost, Woody is a guy struggling to keep his head above the waterline of contemporary life. For someone so thoroughly rooted in today, he seems to find the struggle exceptionally tough. Today just doesn't agree with Woody, whether he's encountering a Neanderthal mugger in the lobby:

> He had just learned to walk erect that morning. He came for me and started to tap-dance on my windpipe. Very quickly I lapsed into the old Navaho Indian trick of screaming and begging. Finally, about six cops came; they saw what was going on, and took his side.

or a ritzy new hairdryer:

> It was my wife's birthday, and we used to exchange novelty gifts all the time. So I bought her, in a Third Avenue antique shop, an electric chair. Told her it was a hairdryer. It blew out all the lights in the house, y'know, but it gave her a great tan.

Whether it also dried her hair is anyone's guess!

As a loser in love, Woody is unable to achieve the adultery which New York State requires for a divorce. Asked to do him a favor by committing adultery with him, one girl refuses, declaring: "Not even if it would help the

24

space program!" Eventually his wife obliges. He dreams of bachelor bliss. He imagines returning to the glories of Life Before Marriage when he misbehaved with passionate secretaries at drunken office parties. The centerpiece of his fantasies is the bachelor pad with wall-to-wall air hostesses, running amok, day and night. Although he has become a little out of touch during his years of abstemious marriage he is, he is convinced, "basically a stud."

His patter moves effortlessly from one subject to another, constantly settling on the self-disparaging image: "I don't know how many of you out there noticed... I do not have a stock theatrical suntan. I'm redheaded and fair-skinned. I don't tan, I stroke."

Allen is always disarmingly casual about the most personal aspects of his character and experiences. Neither as a stand-up comic nor as a screen actor has he ever needed the obligatory mother-in-law to score points off — Woody Allen has Woody Allen.

> I was in analysis, you should know that about me. I was in group analysis when I was younger, 'cos I couldn't afford private. I was captain of the latent paranoids softball team. We used to play all the neurotics on Sunday morning; the nailbiters against the bedwetters!

Much of Woody Allen's magic lies in his subtlety, in his understanding of the kind of audience we are or would like to think we are. We're smart, and think we're even smarter, and we're prepared to work a little for our laughs. Occasionally, Woody responds by allowing us to supply our own punchlines:

> We did a play in acting class by Paddy Chayevsky called *Gideon.* I played the part of God — typecasting. It was Method acting, so two weeks beforehand I started to live the part offstage, and I really came on Godly. I was fabulous. I put on a blue suit. I took taxicabs all over New York, I tipped big, 'cos He would have. Some guy hit my fender and I said unto him: "Be fruitful... and multiply!"... though not in those words.

As well as being the most cerebral comic, he is also the most literary. After making fun of jazz and philosophy it is predictable that he would trash the world of books. In one devastating routine he makes fun of several of America's most legendary novelists, although he is clearly not attacking their literature so much as the reputations and myths which surround the books.

> I mentioned before that I was in Europe. It's not the first time that I was in Europe. I was in Europe many years ago with Ernest Hemingway. Hemingway had just written his first novel and Gertrude Stein and I read it and we said it was a good novel but not a great one, and that it needed some work, but it could be a fine book. And we laughed over it, and Hemingway punched me in the mouth.
> I remember Scott and Zelda Fitzgerald came home from their *wild* New Year's party. It was April, Scott had just written "Great Expectations" and Gertrude Stein and I read it and we said it was a good book but there was no need to have written it because Charles Dickens had already written it. And we laughed over it, and Hemingway punched me in the mouth.
> That winter we went to Spain to see Manoleté fight. He looked to me 18 and Gertrude Stein said No, he was 19, but that he only looked 18 and I said sometimes a boy of 18 will look 19 whereas other times a 19 year old will only look 18. That's the way it is with a true Spaniard. We laughed over that, and Gertrude Stein punched me in the mouth. Then the war came. Hemingway went to Africa to do a book, and Gertrude Stein moved in with Alice Toklas and I went to New York to see my orthodontist.

Allen's material is not conceived as written prose, but as talk. The spoken word seems far more lively and spontaneous. More real. It has a lot more nuance and personality, as Woody appears to ramble, digress, interrupt himself, add afterthoughts, and, occasionally, refer back to an earlier funny line. His spiel sounds loose and freewheeling. He seems to bubble along, chattering away, apparently off the top of his head. His stuff is chatter, but it is the most beautifully *exact* chatter of any stand-up comedian. It is artfully structured and precise in a way which allows his gags to link, build, accumulate and explode. His patter is more carefully written than a lot of prose, and in the rhythms of exposition and punchline he is a master.

> I'm gonna tell a love story now. This occured before I was married, a long time ago, in Manhattan, this was at City Center, ages ago. I was watching a ballet at City Center. I'm not a ballet fan at all, but they were doing The Dying Swan. There was a rumor that

some bookmakers had drifted into town from upstate New York, that they had fixed the ballet. Apparently there was a lot of money bet on the swan to live...

And I look in the box and I see a girl — and my weak spot is women — I always think some day they're gonna make me a birthday party and wheel out a tremendous birthday cake, and a giant naked woman is gonna leap out of the cake and hurt me, and leap back in. So I pick up this girl, I was very glib. She was a brilliant girl, she was a Bennington girl, studying at Bennington to be a woman male nurse, a four year program, working on a term paper on the increasing incidence of heterosexuality among homosexuals.

In any decade, this is sparkling stuff. Even in 1964, Woody Allen was already an accomplished comic artist. Having started out writing individual gags, he was now writing routines, quick little stories which contain a clever series of related gags. One of the best remembered of these is his exceptionally clever and sustained moose routine:

I shot a moose once. I was hunting in upstate New York, and I shot a moose and I strap him onto the fender of my car and I'm driving home along the West Side Highway, but what I didn't realize was that the bullet did not penetrate the moose. It just creased his scalp, knocking him unconscious. And I'm driving through the Holland Tunnel and the moose woke up. So I'm driving with a live moose on my fender... and the moose is signalling... and there's a law in New York State against driving with a conscious moose on your fender... Tuesdays, Thursdays and Saturdays... and I'm *very panicky*... then it hits me. Some friends of mine are having a costume party: I'll go, I'll take the moose, I'll ditch him at the party, it wouldn't be my responsibility.

So I drive up to the party, I knock on the door, the moose is next to me. My host comes to the door. I say "Hello, you know the Solomons?" We enter. The moose mingles very well... scored... some guy was trying to sell him insurance for an hour and a half. 12 o'clock comes. They give out prizes for the best costume of the night. First prize goes to the Berkowitzes, a married couple dressed as a moose.

Woody's delivery gets faster, more excited, manic:

> The moose comes in second. *The moose is furious!* He and the Berkowitzes lock antlers in the living room. They knock each other unconscious. Now, I figure, here's my chance, I grab the moose, strap him on my fender, shoot back to the woods... But!... I've got the Berkowitzes!!! So I'm driving along with two Jewish people on my fender... There's a law in New York State... Tuesdays, Thursdays and *especially* Saturdays... the following morning the Berkowitzes wake up in the woods in a moose suit. Mr Berkowitz is shot, stuffed and mounted at the New York Athletic Club and the joke is on them 'cos IT'S RESTRICTED!!!

# Print Sprints

If one didn't have the collections of writings *Getting Even* and *Without Feathers,* it would be easier to relegate Allen to some minor position in the sub-strata of American comedy, but with those brilliant parodies and uncharted flights-of-fancy, one has seriously to consider him alongside names like Kaufman, Perelman and Benchley; and he may well produce a full-scale novel in the near future.
Charles Marowitz, 1977

Mr Marowitz is an accomplished critic and theater director, but you have to disagree with him. Woody Allen is no author. Among successful comedians he is uniquely literate and serious, but he is not a great humorous writer. He is a comedian who can write funny articles.

Prose fiction is not his bag. What should he do? Lock himself in a room for five years and try to write a better novel than *Catch-22*? It's not what he does best. A short humorous piece is a sprint and in this he's world class. But a novel isn't a sprint, it's a marathon and it seems he can't go the distance.

In his writings, Woody's obsession with his intellectual and physical inferiority is at its height. The feeling of being overwhelmed by clever women is a recurrent theme. In *Getting Even,* his first collection, one of his heroes, Weinstein says "His problem was women, and he knew it. He was impotent with any woman who finished college with higher than a B-minus average. He felt most at home with graduates of the typing school, although if the woman did over 60 words a minute he panicked and could not perform."

A similar notion recurs in *The Whore Of Mensa*. In this Woody has had a very ingenious basic idea and developed it into a seven-page story with wonderful descriptions and dialogue. The style is hard-boiled, laconic and fast-moving. It is told in the first person by Kaiser, a private eye who is visited in his office by a traveling salesman who explains that he needs the stimulus of contact with brainy women: "I mean, my wife is great, don't get me wrong. But she won't discuss Pound with me. Or Eliot. I didn't know that when I married her. See, I need a woman who's mentally stimulating, Kaiser. And I'm willing to pay for it. I don't want an involvement — I want a quick intellectual experience, then I want the girl to leave, Christ, Kaiser, I'm a happily married man."

He recounts how he became the victim of a team of educated call-girls, masterminded by a Madame Flossie, who visit customers for intellectual titillation. One of the girls is blackmailing him. She has a tape of them discussing *The Waste Land* in a motel room. She wants ten grand or she'll play the tape to his wife.

Kaiser takes the case. He phones Flossie and orders a girl to come over to a room in the Plaza Hotel to discuss Melville. Soon, Sherry arrives, "a young redhead who was packed into her slacks like two big scoops of vanilla ice cream." They rap; he lays a C-note on her; then he flashes his badge and says he's the fuzz. She breaks down and confesses that she's a struggling student who needs the money to finish her thesis:

> It all poured out — the whole story. Central Park West upbringing. Socialist summer camps. Brandeis. She was every dame you saw waiting in line at the Elgin or the Thalia, or penciling the words "Yes, very true" into the margin of some book on Kant. Only somewhere along the line she had made a wrong turn.

She's been busted twice before, once for reading *Commentary* in a parked car. Tough but understanding, Kaiser takes pity and lets her off. He visits the bookstore which is a front for the "brothel", and in a swift denouement, grabs the gun from Flossie, who turns out to be a man, calls police HQ and wraps up the case.

*The Whore of Mensa* is original, pacy, stylish and hilarious. By any standards, it is an exceptional piece of comic writing, perhaps the funniest and most sustained piece in any collection. It is exactly the right length, neither too short to rob us of the enjoyment of a scenario worth savoring, nor too long to make us think Woody was enjoying his own ingenuity too much, although we can easily imagine him giggling delightedly over his typewriter.

If only all his pieces were as brilliant.

It should be said that his prose style is nothing like S.J. Perelman's. In print Woody is taut, modern, journalistic. He is never florid. Where Perelman is an orchestral genius who conducts a symphony of words, Woody is a journeyman fiddler who knows some good tunes. If Perelman is the Nabokov of short humorous pieces. Allen is more like the Ed McBain: while the style of the former is distinguished by the virtuosity of what he puts in, that of the other is characterized by what is left out.

Symphonic Sid spins fantastically beautiful prose, making words dance magically through inspired and dazzling digressions, entrancing himself with the fertility of his imagination, and with his voluminous range of reference. By comparison the sentences Woody chops out are more akin to those of a good procedural police thriller from the 87th Precinct. Woody admits that his early writings were heavily influenced by Perelman. A typical SJP essay will often start with a very long sentence, and even in his more restrained openings there are hints of the elegant garrulousness to come. Consider this intro from Perelman's masterly *Crazy Like A Fox:*

> It is always something of a shock to approach a newsstand which handles trade publications and find the Corset And Underwear Review displayed next to the American Bee Journal. However, newsstands make strange bedfellows, as anyone who has ever slept with a newsstand can testify, and if you think about it at all (instead of sitting there in a torpor with your mouth half open) you'd see this proximity is not only alphabetical. Both the Corset And Underwear Review and American Bee Journal are concerned with honeys: although I am beast enough to prefer a photograph of a succulent nymph in satin Lastex Girdleiere with Thrill Plus Bra to the most dramatic snapshot of an apiary, each has its place in my scheme.

Among humorists. Perelman is an arrogant aristocrat who enjoys his

genius and flaunts it, taunting the reader with his superiority. His tone is supercilious. Woody is often as fanciful, but his prose is much more down-to-earth. His most Perelmanesque opening salvo is in *Yes, But Can The Steam Engine Do This?:*

> I was leafing through a magazine while waiting for Joseph K., my beagle to emerge from his regular Tuesday fifty minute hour with a Park Avenue therapist — a Jungian vetinarian who, for fifty dollars per session labors valiantly to convince him that jowls are not a social drawback — when I came across a sentence at the bottom of the page that caught my eye like an overdraft notice.

The style gets plainer as the piece goes on, with the narrator fantasizing about the item which reveals the stunning news that the sandwich was invented by the Earl of Sandwich. He reconstructs highlights from the life of this underappreciated innovator, such as:

> 1741: Living in the country on a small inheritance, he works day and night, often skimping on meals to save money for food. His first completed work — a slice of bread, a slice of bread on top of that, and a slice of turkey on top of both — fails miserably. Bitterly disappointed, he returns to his studio and begins again.

Another highlight from *Getting Even* concerns postal chess and is titled *The Gossage-Vardebian Papers.* It is written in the form of an exchange of letters, nine in all. In his first letter, Gossage claims that one of his knights being taken 23 moves ago was due to a move he posted being lost in the mail. From then on the correspondence is aflame with the most appalling lies, cheating, gamesmanship and sarcasm. Both men are obviously lunatics. It has to be admitted that this piece is of limited appeal, and perhaps incomprehensible to people who do not play chess. But then that tends to be Woody's audience: people who play a bit of chess, and know their way round jazz, literature and foreign films.

*A Twenties Memory* is a return to that other Allen obsession, the intelligentsia: the bright and brainy lights, usually screened from ridicule by the intensity with which they take themselves seriously. It is full of clever lines and inspired silliness: "Picasso was a short man who had a funny way of walking by putting one foot in front of the other until he would take what he called 'steps' " and "Dali decided to have a one-man show which he did,

*At home with his fantasies.*

and it was a huge success as one man showed up."

Woody is an educated comedian, not a scholar. Because he was no aca-demic, and knew you don't have to be a student to read books, he dropped out of college to write jokes for comedians. Being self-educated, and frivo-lous by nature and profession, he inevitably makes fun of intellectuals, and the concerns of intellectuals. In *My Philosophy,* he recounts how he started reading the major western thinkers during a month's convales-cence in hospital, following a domestic accident in which his wife dropped a spoonful of her home-made soufflé on his foot.

Within the traditions of Jewish humor, Woody has staked out his own ter-ritory, or territories. He cracks jokes about the kind of things no one else makes jokes about. Who else would write: "He had been a precocious child. An intellectual. At twelve he had translated the poems of T.S. Eliot into English after some vandals had broken into the library and translated them into French."

Sometimes his style in print is uncannily like his style with the spoken word. Consider the following: "It was no use. Rien à rire, rien à faire. Weinstein left and walked over to Union Square. Suddenly tears burst forth. Hot salty tears pent up for ages rushed out in an unabashed wave of emotion. The problem was, they were coming out of his ears. Look at this, he thought: I can't even cry properly. He dabbed his ear with a Kleenex and went home." This is prose which resembles talk. It has the same rhythm and sentence-structure as a chunk from one of Woody's stand-up routines. As you read it, you can hear his voice.

Other pieces are not prose but playlets like *God (A Play)* and *Death (A Play)* which deal with the Big Questions which are (surprise, surprise) Death and God. In another short play called *Death Knocks,* Nat Ackerman, an old garment manufacturer, is visited at midnight by Death who agrees to play gin rummy with Nat. If Death wins, Nat has to go with him there and then, but if Nat wins he lives another day. So he wins, of course, and Death has to come back the next night.

Obviously, Woody is renowned for his one-liners. Clever lines are often funnier in conversation than they are on paper. When two or more people are talking, a one-liner can stab, interrupt and surprise. It is a verbal gun-shot, straight from the lip. But developing clever lines into sentences which become paragraphs which become pages which become humorous pieces is another game entirely. Some of his pieces are merely a suc-cession of fragments, a series of unlinked paragraphs containing remarks and observations on this and that.

Health is a frequent concern of comedians, and Woody is, or pretends to be, an imaginative hypochondriac. In one lively piece, *A little Louder Please,* he takes a pose as a culture critic and commentator:

> It began one day last January when I was standing in McGinnis' bar on Broadway, engulfing a slab of the world's richest cheese-cake and suffering the guilty cholesterolish hallucination that I could hear my aorta congealing into a hockey puck.

Later in the same piece comes a classic example of the kind of character vignette that was a highlight of Woody's stage routines. In context, it is de-livered in a throwaway style, preceded by perhaps the ultimate throwaway on the topic of prowess with women. The narrator (for which read Woody) has just been handed two free tickets to an evening of off-Broadway theatrics.

> I was unable to get a date on only six weeks notice, so I used the extra ticket to tip my window-washer, Lars, a lethargic menial with all the sensitivity of the Berlin Wall. At first he thought the little orange pasteboard was edible, but when I explained that it was good for an evening of pantomine — one of the only spectator events outside of a fire that he could hope to understand — he thanked me profusely.

That a gag-writer and comedian should publish quality humor pieces is unusual. That he should publish most of them in The New Yorker is remark-able. Eleven of the seventeen pieces collected in *Getting Even* were pub-lished originally in The New Yorker, that scrupulously-edited weekly maga-zine which has long been regarded as the guardian of certain traditions of cartooning, criticism and fiction. The written word is sacred here, in the bastion of metropolitan literary sophistication.
A fabulous gallery of immortals has graced its pages: Dorothy Parker, Irwin Shaw, Nabokov, Thurber, O'Hara, Salinger, Cheever, Updike, Ca-pote. Indeed Updike once admitted: "From the age of twelve when my aunt gave us a subscription for Christmas, The New Yorker has seemed to me the best of possible magazines and their acceptance of a poem and story by me in June of 1954 remains the ecstatic breakthrough of my literary life. Their editorial care, and their gratitude for a piece of work they like, are incomparable."

For Woody Allen to make it here must have been bliss. Here, in columns of print flanked by ads for Waterford crystal and $6000 Swiss watches and imported liqueurs and Scandinavian fox fur coats and luxury tennis holidays in Bermuda and Bulova Quartz Travel Alarms, a cab-driver's son from Brooklyn was addressing the smartest, most civilized readers in America!

# Video Vaudeville

High-rolling producer Charles K. Feldman discovered Woody at the Blue
Angel Club in New York and hired him to write the screenplay for Clive
Donner's *What's New, Pussycat?* in 1965.

This was a wild! zany! Swinging Sixties! extravaganza which was supposed to be The Marx Bros - meets-the-Beatles. Peter Sellers played a
deranged psychiatrist, and while he and Woody can't seem to score, fashion editor Peter O'Toole has fun with girls like Romy Schneider,
Paula Prentiss as a stripper-poetess, Capucine as a knockabout model,
and Ursula Andress as an Amazonian type in a snakeskin catsuit.

An American film directed by an Englishman, *What's New Pussycat?* was
heavily influenced by *Help, Hard Day's Night* and *The Knack,* three English films directed by an American, Dick Lester. Unfortunately, it was
drivel. The critics panned it, but it did well at the box-office. Woody knew it
was garbage, but it was a start in films. Later, he appeared in *Casino
Royale,* also produced by Feldman.

In this period he made many TV appearances, and wrote two hit comedies
for Broadway, *Don't Drink The Water,* and *Play It Again, Sam* in which he
also starred. Another project which showed that in the Sixties his imagination was swinging as wildly as anyone's was *What's Up, Tiger Lily.* This
was a cheapo Japanese spy flick, a 007 spoof, which Woody acquired the

American rights to, redubbed with witty dialogue and released successfully in the US.

Film is a collaborative medium, and the chemistry of a collaboration is sometimes elusive, to say the least. Different films get put together in different ways. Actor-producers like Robert Redford and Warren Beatty may get a screenplay and cast together before looking around for a director. Producers may tailor a script for a star who drops out, so another star comes in who wants another director. Big name screenwriters can find themselves working on a rewrite of a rewrite of a rewrite. Sometimes this process can be spread over several years. And however keen the originators of a project are to see it completed it usually needs a determination bordering on obsession.

Clearly, anyone who can perform several of the essential functions has fewer people to collaborate with, and, in theory fewer obstacles. Starting as a writer and performer, Woody Allen has emerged steadily as a self-employed, self-obsessed comic artist, working steadily to define, refine, and re-define his vision, and to bring it to the screen. What's up there is the world according to Woody.

In a decade of director-worship like the Seventies, Woody benefited from the trend. We seemed to be living in the age of director-as-superstar. We heard more and more about author-tycoons such as Altman, Spielberg and Coppola, the "Movie Brats" as they came to be called. As Billy Wilder remarked, the kids with beards have taken over. The leading practitioners of comedy were Elaine May, Mel Brooks and Woody, all of whom are writer-actor-directors. They proved that the do-it-yourself approach can be the source of exceptionally funny films, and in recent years Alan Alda has taken a leaf out of their book and started writing and directing.

Clearly, being an actor is far more frustrating than being a writer. An actor has to wait for other people, and depend on them. He waits for the phone to ring, he auditions, and if he's religious, he prays someone will give him a part. Director Paul Mazursky talked about this to John Higgins in The Times when he was interviewed about his film *Next Stop, Greenwich Village,* a story of a struggling young comedian in the Fifties who tries to shake off his family ties. He said he began by trying to be an actor: "During those early days I had a go at everything. I was an actor, I was a director in a small way, I was even a night club comic for five years. The trouble was that in none of those various roles was I particularly successful. And I soon realized that one of the most humiliating, boring and frustrating things was to be an actor who is constantly being offered small parts, if he is given any

*In his Manhattan apartment. Triple thick shakes all round.*

parts at all."

Woody has made a point of avoiding appearing in other people's films. Occasionally, however, it is possible that he can be persuaded to star in someone else's film, if the subject appeals to him, which was the case with *The Front.*

Directed by Martin Ritt, this concerned the Red Scare of the Fifties, when suspected communists were cruelly blacklisted and prevented from working in movies, TV and radio. They were hounded and persecuted by the notorious House of Representatives Unamerican Activities Committee.

Victims who were actors went abroad, or into the theater. Directors like Jules Dassin and Joseph Losey went to work in France and Britain. Writers sold scripts under false names or through front men, who claimed authorship. Many excellent writers refused to collaborate with the Committee, including Dashiell Hammett, Irwin Shaw, Lillian Hellman, Ring Lardner Jr and Dalton Trumbo. The story of *The Front,* Hollywood's first attempt to exorcise these phantoms from the early Fifties, is set not in Los Angeles but around the New York television scene in 1950. At that time Walter Bernstein and actor Martin Ritt were respectively author and actor in a big live TV series, and were among those blacklisted.

Obviously, this is marvellous material for a movie. The whole moral, political and psychological implications of these events provides an ideal context for a powerful film. But after 25 years of waiting, and many years of trying to find finance for such a controversial subject, Ritt blew it by holding back. He delivered an intelligent film which lacks passion and is, ultimately, a missed opportunity.

Allen tends a cash register in a bar. He ferries illegal bets, and loses most of the time. He is a failure, not the normal Woody Allen failure — a social and sexual disaster area — but simply chaotic, even dumb, though capable of the cleverly-flighted *faux nair* remarks.

One of his friends is a TV script writer (Michael Murphy) who has been blacklisted and cannot work. He comes to Woody with the offer of 10 per cent of all profits if Woody can sell his material. This he does with great success; Woody waltzes in happily once a week with 'his' scripts and the goods are snapped up. He is soon embarrassing himself with the close attentions of a shapely script editor (Andrea Marcovicci) until he himself is hauled up before the fearsome HUAC members and asked to spell out his allegiances.

*The Front* invites a great deal of laughter, but Allen this time is a comic actor rather than a comedian. There are glimpses of the perpetual victim but there are also some well-handled straight dramatic moments in which the victim persona confronts the hard truths he can't wisecrack his way around. It's a somewhat different Allen, but a good and efficient Allen.

The critics were mostly sympathetic. Alan Brien expressed reservations but found it "an extraordinary, individual and inventive entertainment." David Robinson, reviewing the film at length concluded that *"The Front* is wise, literate, witty, intelligently played (notably by Woody Allen in an impressive debut as a straight man, and by the graceful Andrea Marcovicci): yet it is melancholy and muted where it should, even today, be angry. The role played by Zero Mostel seems symptomatic. Blacklisted in 1950 Mostel was celebrated for the belligerence of his resistance. (At his hearing in 1955 he wiggled five fingers to indicate he was invoking the Fifth Amendment; and at the conclusion of his televised testimony formally thanked the committee 'for making it possible for me to be on television since I've been blacklisted from it for the past five years.')

In the Chicago Tribune under the headline "Woody and mirth upstage the message", Gene Siskel saw the movie in a different light, "A mistake in casting destroys what *The Front* would like to be — and turns it into a frequently funny picture about a serious subject.

*Dinner for one in What's New Pussycat?*

A casting mistake can do all that?

Yes it can, at least when the miscast one is comedian Woody Allen.

*The Front* is not the newest Woody Allen comedy. At least that's the message Columbia Pictures and Woody Allen want you to believe."

This sort of attitude is easy to understand when you think of some of the typical Allen one-liners that shoot out unexpectedly from the gloom and stab you in the rib cage.

She: I'm from Connecticut

He: Oh, very fancy

She: Yes, I'm from a very proper family. The kind of family where the worst thing you could do was talk too loud

He: The worst thing you could do in my family was to buy retail

The incongruity of the joke only helped to overshadow the ensuing destruction of the career of TV Comic Heckey Brown already half-lost beneath a barrage of previous guffaws.

Allen himself had been drawn to *The Front* by among other things his preference for serious drama; it was the chance of a role on a different level from what he had yet experienced. That didn't stop doubts though.

"Suppose you get Peter Falk instead of me?" he pleaded with director Martin Ritt a few days before his debut and added shortly before the premiere.

"I decided to take a chance. From the beginning, I had enormous reservations about doing a film which I had not written and over which I would have no directorial control. I wasn't sure how I would feel being a hired actor in a dramatic movie, and I said 'if you want a guy to make conversation, hire Jack Nicholson. I felt uncomfortable throughout the whole process, not being able to improvise and change things. And I could never judge how things were going. My only yardstick is funniness!"

The ambivalence that Woody felt about his own rôle in *The Front* was shared by Russell Davies who wrote, "The problem with the picture is not that Allen has taken on a 'serious' role that is too much for him, but, on the contrary, that director Martin Ritt has made him feel too much at home. As the political climax is reached, Woody is still funny — jarringly funny — so that his final clash with the Committee is not felt to be an historical self-sacrifice, but merely the culminating gesture in a comedy performance. You may be sure Ritt has thought his own attitudes out deeply. For both he and his writer Walter Bernstein were on the blacklist themselves. But in the event, both men seem to have avoided drawing the bitterest conclusions from the events of the early Fifties."

# Dump the rushes and run

*Take The Money And Run* (1969) from a screenplay by Allen and Mickey Rose, with Allen, Janet Margolin, Marcel Hillaire, Jacquelyn Hyde, and Lonny Chapman. A spoof of crime and prison movies, this one has several anthology gags like the bank hold-up note none of the tellers can read, but also many over-worked concepts like the shamed parents wearing masks for television interviews.
Village Voice

In his excellent book *When The Shooting Stops... The Cutting Begins* film editor Ralph Rosenblum describes how his path crossed with Woody's in 1969.

The circumstances surrounding their first meeting were far from ideal. Ralph got a phone call from production manager Jack Grossberg asking him to come and see *Take The Money And Run* which was finished but distinctly unsatisfactory. After eight months in the cutting room it was a gangster spoof complete with titles, sound effects and music, starring Woody as a timid crook, Virgil Starkwell.

Rosenblum encountered a massive cloud of depression and anxiety surrounding the project. The film had been screened many times privately, and had always died: no laughter. Everyone was demoralized. They were

43

talking about not releasing it. Better to have a flop in private than a flop in public. Night club comedian tries to direct film, fails, end of story, thank you and goodnight.

The editor describes the version he saw as "a film that seemed to be flying all over the place, with highs as high as the Marx Brothers and lows as low as a slapped-together home movie." It was a mixture of inspiration and amateurism, and no one liked the ending.

"The film was packed with funny material. It was frenetic and formless and obviously the work of a very fresh mind. But even as I was enjoying it, I began to feel that it was going on forever. The whole thing was put together in a strange inept way with little rhythm and a very bad sense of continuity. Whoever made it had no sense of film pace: it would rush along and then stop, then rush along and then stop again. Truly comic incidents were murdered by weak cuts, awkward juxtapositions, excessive length or lack of completion."

As if this wasn't bad enough, Rosenblum felt the film contained too many moments of totally inappropriate pathos and seriousness. Also, Woody's violent death at the end was a turn-off: escaping from a bank robbery, he is gunned down by the police. Blood spurting everywhere. Carnage. The final shot was of his bloodstained body.

Rosenblum did not know if he could rescue the film. The scale and complexity of the re-editing required was somewhat intimidating, as was the level of paranoia which surrounded the project. Stalling, he asked to see the script, in which he was amazed to find many jokes which were not in the movie. He was assured that all of these had been filmed, plus others which Woody had improvised on the set.

He recalls how he met Woody for the first time in a seafood restaurant, and liked him. Woody was going to be away from New York for several months, touring with *Play It Again, Sam.* They agreed that the editor should have all the original footage, 200 boxes of it, delivered to his office. "For the following two weeks I screened a collection of skits that were so original, so charming, so funny in absolutely unexpected ways that it made this period one of the most pleasurable in all my years of editing. A publisher stumbling upon the unpublished notebooks of a young Robert Benchley might have felt similarly."

There were many surprises. "I found that Woody had shot about a half dozen endings for the movie, all of them sentimental, weakly amusing or sad. I told him that we had to shoot a new end — a demand that I would repeat on three of our next four films together."

*An autograph hunter strikes gold.*

He began to reconstruct the film, removing the dead spots, trying to give it shape, rhythm and pace. Many of the discarded jokes were wonderful, but flawed; the experienced editor knew how they could be used to make the film longer and better. "I put back some scenes, extended or recut others, juggling the material to create a rhythm, which in some cases meant removing whole scenes from one part of the film to another, and trimming almost everything to quicken the pace."

There were many glorious, but brief, sketches. Attempting to rob a pet shop, Woody is chased out by a gorilla; his girlfriend visits him in prison, and presses a hard-boiled egg through the grille; as a child he is seen being beaten up by neighborhood thugs who smash his cello; in one more complex scene his gang plan to rob a bank while pretending to shoot a film; in a prison break-out he uses a replica pistol painstakingly sculptured from soap and colored black with shoe polish, but an unexpected shower of rain causes his "gun" to foam up into a handful of suds.

In one classic and farcical sequence, Woody perpetrates his first bank job.

He gives a note to the teller who can't read it so he calls a second teller who can't read it either, and eventually they figure out it's a stick-up but they can't give him any money without the vice-president's initials, and the people in the line behind Woody are complaining and Woody says he's in a hurry... and in the last shot he is in custody, making his one phone call.

In linking and cementing scenes and building continuity, Rosenblum took a brilliant but mostly unused long interview with Virgil's parents, chopped it up, and used it to join otherwise awkward pieces of action. In one scene he changed the music to ragtime and magically transformed the visuals from sad to funny. The changes in the score meant more work for a struggling young composer who, until hired to score *Take The Money,* had been working mostly as a rehearsal pianist: Marvin Hamlisch.

In this, his first venture as director, Woody could not resist sending up a reasonably recent dramatic film. Ten years earlier Tony Curtis and Sidney Poitier had escaped from a chain-gang in *The Defiant Ones.* The fugitive pair were chained together at the ankle. Where most people saw social comment and symbolism, Woody's comic imagination saw something else. He has his hero Virgil and four other prisoners, one of them black, break out of prison camp chained together, chased across country by dogs and guards and (cutting a long story short) stealing four bicycles. We see four chained convicts cycling away down a country road with Woody, also chained, jogging alongside!

The editor attributes the dead spots to Woody's obsessive desire to keep a strain of seriousness in the film. This clown did not want to play the Prince of Denmark, he wanted to play the king of Swedish filmmakers, and years later, he did. As Rosenblum comments: "His enduring need to communicate emotional anguish finally surfaced in the form of the indisputably sombre *Interiors,* but during the making of *Take The Money* the gravity was strictly in the way."

The Allen-Rosenblum collaboration was to last ten years. As he notes in a chapter titled Scenes From a Marriage: "It was certainly rewarding for me to contribute to the films of a man whose struggles I identified with and whose material I liked and respected. And I believe it was comforting for Woody, who feels so out of step with the world, to work with someone who understood his references, values, tastes and anxieties."

# Yes, we have bananas

Woody packed *Bananas* so full of jokes that another movie could have been made from its outtakes. If he thought he needed 150 jokes in an hour and a half, he wrote and photographed 300. And he made them tighter, a joke at every turn, so that the pace would never slacken.
Ralph Rosenblum.

*Bananas* opens with a spoof of streetfighting-as-a-spectator-sport. It's a Wide World Of Sports report on the colorful and exciting riot finals with real-life sportcaster Howard Cosell saying "Let me through, this is American television!" He goes over to interview the new dictator.

Then comes the credit sequence with the usual names of his team (Ralph Rosenblum, editor, and Charles Joffe, executive producer, and so on) and bullet holes appearing in the screen.

Woody plays Fielding Mellish, a products-tester for a large corporation, his most blue-collar role. We first see him at work on the Execusizer, an ingenious piece of equipment for the fitness-conscious but deskbound executive. Instead of a chair, he has a cycling machine, and spring-loaded telephones which are like chest-expanders. There is a basketball hoop above a filing cabinet which swallows and regurgitates scoring shots.

In the establishing scenes we soon see the familiar lonely misfit. We see

49

him knock off and go in to see Norma, a secretary who says she is having some friends over to show porno movies tonight, but doesn't invite him. In a newsagent shop he ogles an assortment of girlie magazines. An old lady eyes him disapprovingly. He buys Time, Newsweek, Commentary and, furtively, one adult publication whose title we cannot see. The cashier is unsure of the price of this one and calls loudly across the shop to his assistant: "Hey Ralph, how much is a copy of Orgasm?"

In many sequences of *Bananas* there is no dialogue, just music. A honky tonk piano plays in a subway scene where our weak and weedy protagonist is mauled and thumped by two leather-jacketed delinquents, one of whom is played by a very young Sylvester Stallone.

Back home at his apartment a blond canvasser (Louise Lasser) knocks on his door with a petition. He snaps her pencil point and invites her in. We know we are in for some silly conversational sparring. Woody is the poet laureate of embarrassed exploratory smalltalk. His screen character is typically a social imbecile who perches precariously on every conversational tightrope, and this encounter is no exception.

"Have you ever been to Amsterdam?" asks Nancy.

"Oh yeah, I've been to the Vatican."

"But the Vatican's in Rome!"

"Er... they were doing so well in Rome that they opened one in Amsterdam."

Conversations like this do not really reveal character or propel a narrative. They merely set up funny punchlines, and illustrate Woody's mastery of the nuts and bolts of joke-writing. In fact, this particular gag would work almost as well in a monologue as it does here in dialogue, Nancy is a philosophy major at City College. Woody drives a VW. They have a lot in common. Inspired by his new friend, he goes to picket an embassy, a scene of mayhem, chaos and near-strangulation. Soon it is time for the Big Seduction Scene. At his apartment he wears a playboy-type shirt with a horrific yellow floral pattern and hipster-cut slacks. She goes into the bathroom. Left alone for a moment, he panics and tips a huge container of talc down the front of his shirt, so that he looks as if he's been hit by a flour bomb.

We cut to analysis. He is on the couch saying "I was a nervous child, a bedwetter." He recalls a dream he has had many times. The dream is vividly re-enacted for us, a modern crucifixion scene in which he is being carried through New York on a cross by five men in black, hooded monk's robes. They find an empty parking space and move towards it. Just then another squad with another man on another cross arrive and contest the parking space. Like angry motorists the two teams argue, gesticulate, wrestle and brawl.

Meanwhile he is in love with Nancy, but in a park scene she tells him she doesn't want to see him any more. They talk but the scene is lame: it is not convincingly awkward or sad or touching or true. It is just a yawn.

Then he visits his parents, who are surgeons, to tell them he is off to San Marcos. He goes into an operating theater where Mom and Dad are working on a patient whose eyes are open during the operation. From the moment we notice that the patient is conscious we know he will say something, and he does, but it's anti-climatic. The scene fizzles out. What could have been hysterical is only mildly hilarious.

Then the soundtrack goes into folksy Latin music from acoustic guitars and female vocals. We see military types torturing a prisoner by playing him an LP of an operetta. He confesses what he knows of the rebel's plans. Meanwhile, Fielding has arrived in San Marcos, checked into his hotel and is soon invited to dinner by President Vargas. In his room he is surprised to hear harp music. He opens his wardrobe to find a seated man plucking a harp, practicing. It is the kind of sight gag Woody finds hard to resist.

The dinner scene is a room full of evil, greasy men in army uniforms and shades. The president's waiter brings the food, tastes it, OKs it, steps back, falls on the floor, writhes about and crawls away towards the kitchen, completely ignored by the diners. Vargas claims to be immune to poisoning. Illogically, at the end of the meal the waiter brings Fielding the bill, he queries it and after considerable silliness Vargas gives the waiter one of Fielding's credit cards and has the meal charged to his guest! Over brandy the President explains that he has to exterminate a few troublemakers. He cunningly plans to impersonate the rebels, murder Fielding and have the US Government blame the rebels and support his regime.

In a roadside ambush our hero sprints off into the jungle and hides in a river. Dripping wet, but thinking he is safe, he gets KOd from behind by a rifle butt. When he wakes up he finds himself among the real rebels who take him to their jungle HQ. He is informed that Vargas has announced his death, so if he shows up alive he is bound to be killed. Fielding will have to stay with the rebels until the coup, which could be another 18 months.

"But I have a rented car!" he wails.

Fielding joins in with the soldiers. He lines up for lizard stew holding his tin plate; injures himself during hand grenade practice; underachieves in the blindfold rifle-assembly test. Survival techniques he is instructed in include sucking the poison out of snakebites and camouflage lessons with

foliage which makes him look like a tropical shrub, a natural cue for a urination sight gag.

Soon a lady soldier runs through the camp screaming with half her shirt open, holding a naked breast in her cupped palm. "I got bitten by a snake!" she yells. Alerted to the emergency, our hero runs after her. So do all the other soldiers. She is like the Pied Piper, haring through the camp followed by a whole rebel regiment eager to volunteer to guzzle her reptile-stung boob.

The next big scene is the takeaway farce at the jungle deli. Fielding goes into a cafe to order lunch "to go" for everybody, consisting of 1000 grilled cheese sandwiches, 300 tuna fish, 700 regular coffees, 500 cokes and 1000 7-Ups. We see scores of waiters carrying the guerillas' lunch order down jungle trails in dozens of paper sacks, pushing six wheelbarrows full of coleslaw. This sequence, vividly visual and escalating swiftly, is one of the most memorable in the film. Next we see Woody/Fielding flirting with a lady soldier over dinner. As they eat with their fingers their meal becomes more and more sexually suggestive. Finger-licking foreplay. As he takes off his shirt in slow-motion, we wonder what interruption, what fiasco, can prevent him making it with her. None does. He gets laid.

In this film, like his other early efforts, characters appear and disappear, bits are stuck in, and dialogue scenes alternate with visuals-and-music scenes in plots which are so loose as to look more like collages than stories. For example, there is one brief scene inside a troop-carrying plane where the American GIs are talking about their mission.

"Where are we going?"

"San Marcos."

"Who are we fighting for, the Government or the rebels?"

"The CIA are not taking any chances this time, some of us are for and some against."

This is funny, but it is not good filmmaking. It is a cartoon idea which has to be painstakingly and expensively set up once to provide a few moments on celluloid, and one laugh.

The rebels make a successful coup. One by one the leaders of the evil regime are shot by firing squad in one of the nonviolent execution scenes in cinema history. Peckinpah, it ain't. It is announced that the new dictator's rules must be obeyed: "All people will be required to change their underwear every half hour. From now on all underwear will be worn on the outside, so we can check!"

Woody becomes President and flies to the US on a diplomatic mission

*Leaving the pub where*
*he does a regular gig playing*
*clarinet in a jazz band.*

wearing the silliest, falsest red beard imaginable. As he steps out of his limousine a rioting crowd of protesters are barely being contained by uniformed cops. His FBI bodyguards introduce themselves.

"We'll act as your shield against attack," says the security chief. Just then an assailant rushes up and strikes Fielding a fierce blow on the side of the head.

"We missed him," says the FBI man, complacently.

Fielding addresses a dinner. Later his dumb ex-girl Nancy appears but does not recognize him and says how she has always championed his cause. "Could I kiss you once?" she begs. Nancy remarks that he reminds her vaguely of some idiot she used to know. They go to bed. Afterwards, he owns up. "I have a confession to make. I'm Fielding Mellish."

On TV a newscaster previews a few of the day's main stories. Fielding's arrest and trial are among them. Another item trailed is "The National Rifle Association declares Death a good thing."

At the trial, various witnesses are called. A patrolman testifies that Fielding Mellish is a Jewish intellectual drop-out. One of the jurymen is seen to be drinking water through a straw from a goldfish bowl in which a live goldfish is swimming about. As Fielding cross-examines himself, the jurors pass a joint along the front row.

Viewed today, after being tuned to the pace of the M*A*S*H/Rhoda/Soap style of fast-moving TV comedy, this trial scene is colossally slow and boring. Woody asks the empty witness box a question, dashes into it, replies, gets up again to ask himself another question, and so on. He does it four or five times. Once is OK, twice is tedious, and more than twice is torture. It makes one wish he was found guilty. But no: he is acquitted.

The final sequence is an ABC Wide World Of Sports live telecast from the honeymoon suite. Eager fans surround the double bed as we go over to Howard Cosell for a play-by-play description of the action. Woody jogs in boxer-style with a towel round his neck, being massaged by his black trainer. He soon disappears under the bedspread and amid manic undulations and cheers of approval, the marriage is consummated. Radiant, Nancy tells the nation "He's not the worst I've had, but not the best." The groom anticipates their next bout will be in the late Spring. End of intermittently inspired comedy film.

Louise Lasser, who was Woody's second wife, is a comedienne whose engaging, friendly persona was employed to maximum effect by Howard Zieff in *Slither.* She also starred for three years in the soap opera send-up *Mary Hartman, Mary Hartman.*

*Admiring the
scenery backstage
at the Crazy Horse Saloon.*

Rosenblum recalls that originally *Bananas* had a different ending. As the rebel leader, Fielding is invited to give a speech at Columbia University, where he is attacked by a mob of Blacks who want to assassinate him as a gesture to white America. A bomb goes off. Then he climbs out of a pile of sooty rubble with his face black and is mistaken by three Blacks for one of them. Again Ralph told Woody that the end didn't work and asked him if he could think of another ending, preferably one which related to the opening scene. Next day Woody came in with the televised wedding-night-as-prize-fight finale, with spectators, commentary and interviews with the contestants.

Jay Cocks of Time approved of the fun, up to a point. "Allen is an expert practitioner of the scattershot technique, in which anything is attempted for the sake of the gag," he wrote. "Continuity and coherence are early victims of such an approach, but Allen keeps you laughing so steadily that you notice only later that nothing really hangs together or makes much sense at all."

# Forget everything you wanted to know about sex

Messy, tasteless and crazily uneven (as the best talking comedies have often been), the last two pictures he directed — *Bananas* and *Everything You Always Wanted To Know About Sex* — had wild highs that suggested an erratic comic genius.
Pauline Kael, 1973.

Studios and producers like to buy "properties".
For the last 70 years Hollywood Studios have been purchasing best-selling books with catchy titles and then employing teams of writers to devise screenplays to go with them. The properties have included such hot and promising entertainments as 'The Origin of The Species' and 'The Decline Of The West'. In the 1930s MGM even hired S.J. Perelman to make a comedy out of Dale Carnegie's 'How To Win Friends And Influence People!'
In 1971 United Artists bought Dr David Reuben's huge best-seller 'Everything You Always Wanted To Know About Sex But Were Afraid To Ask', and suggested to Woody that he make it into a movie.
The task was impossible, but Woody never shirks a challenge. His film takes the form of a series of seven separate sketches of about ten minutes each. It is supposed to be wild, daring, bizarre, flamboyant and surreal but

*John Carridine as the mad Doctor Bernardo plays the perfect host in Everything You Always Wanted to Know about Sex...*

is, for the most part, stupendously boring. *Sex* is his worst film. It is strictly for people who want to see small men being pursued by mountain-sized breasts, and who like to see Gene Wilder as a doctor whispering sweet nothings into the ear of a sheep wearing a black garter belt. Its 87 minutes seem to last forever. Cut to a 6-minute trailer, it would be funny.

59

*Caught red-handed as
The Fool in Everything You
Always Wanted to Know About Sex...*

# Play it again
# & again & again

*Play It Again, Sam* (1972): Woody Allen incarnating the spirit of Neurotic Love in a funny picture made from his own Broadway hit. He plays a Bogart nut, and most of the film is about hapless girl-chasing. Herbert Ross directs, in a style of suitably loose-limbed laconicism.
The New Yorker.

Given a star and a hit play the money men decided to play safe and hire experienced comedy director Herb Ross.

The film opens with a clip from *Casablanca.* Woody is watching the plane leave with Ingrid Bergman aboard, at the end of the Hollywood classic. Then he goes home to his apartment, a Bogart museum. Stills and movie books everywhere, posters on the wall advertising *Key Largo.*

He is established as Alan, a Bogart fanatic who works for a movie magazine. We see his wife Nancy leaving him, driving away in a Volkswagen. He is a lonely misfit who says he buys TV dinners and sucks them cold. He fantasizes his trench-coated hero Humphrey Bogart advising him on how to treat women. An actual Bogart lookalike appears on the screen (but no one else can see or hear him) and re-appears throughout the film. "There's no secret," says Bogie. "Dames are simple. I never met one who didn't understand a slap in the mouth or a slug from a 45."

In his hour of need his two closest friends come over, a married couple. Dick (Tony Roberts) is a business executive and Linda (Diane Keaton) is a short-haired, tomboyish model, a neurotic hypochondriac who says things like "I'm experiencing a wave of insecurity."

Alan is one of life's victims, always menaced by furniture and machinery, even in his own home. As he opens the medicine cabinet, small bottles rain out on his head. His attempts to use the hairdryer almost wreck the bathroom. His paranoia is so advanced that he soon imagines Nancy easy-riding with a husky Hells Angel-type on a powerful motorbike. He habitually fantasizes the worst disasters and humiliations. Another time he has an imaginary conversation with his ex-wife:

"What's the matter with me, Nancy?"

"Your're a dreamer. You're awkward, you're clumsy, they can see how desperate you are."

"Tonight, that girl? I was toying with her!"

"Face it Alan, you may be very sweet but you're just not sexy."

"Don't be so sure. You never said that when we were married."

"I was thinking it."

The loyal Dick and Linda are being suitably supportive. They fix him up on a blind date with Sharon, a friend of theirs. He is excited and resolves to brush all his teeth. He rushes round dressing the apartment with open books to impress her. Bogart tells him to lay off the aftershave.

Dick and Linda and Sharon come round for a drink at his apartment before they all go out to dinner. As Sharon tells how she was the only girl in a film called Gangbang, the nervous Alan puts on a display of imbecilic incompetence, accidentally flinging albums across the room. Linda tries to explain to her that her date is "a bit tense", while Dick, a business-junkie, phones his office to leave a number where he can be reached.

In one silent scene, with musical accompaniment, he is on the curb trying to catch a cab. One pulls in to deposit three passengers. One by one they get out, passing a joint to him and to each other, and leave. Alan gets into the cab. It remains parked. It is filled with marijuana smoke, so he jumps out coughing, spluttering and choking. This is slapstick for the Woodstock generation, a funny sketch but not one which is integral to this story. It could slot easily into almost any of his early films.

In an art gallery Linda encourages him to talk to a promising brunette who turns out to be a zombie, a pretentious bore. Then the pair decide to take him to the beach for a weekend so he can meet girls. In the car he moans

"I don't tan, I stroke."
Yes, Woody uses a joke he's been using for seven years. The trouble with jokes is this: a new joke is one you have never heard before. And an old joke is one you've heard once. This "stroke" line was good in 1964 and is funny here. After all, most people who saw the film had not seen him in a club, or heard the album.
When Alan and Linda go to the disco in the evening he is a wallflower, a

*"Bogie where are you?" Woody seeks the advice of his mentor as he grapples with a figment of his imagination in Play It Again Sam.*

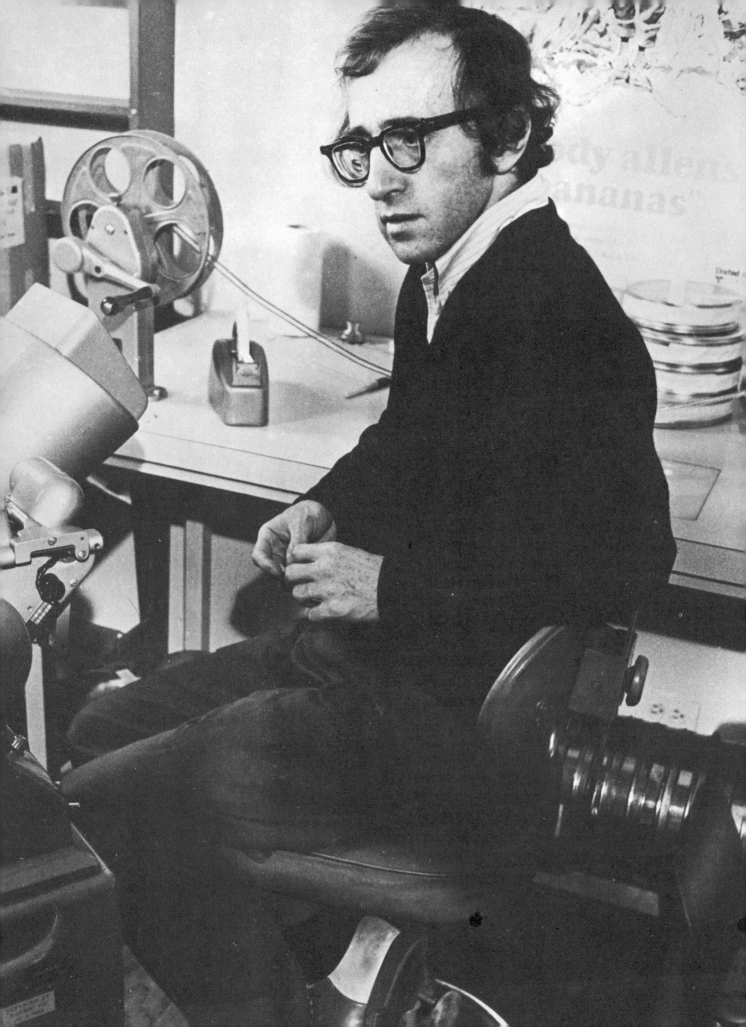

voyeur, only dancing with his friend's wife. He fancies a busty blonde and eyes her longingly, and encouraged by matchmaker Linda, he eventually works up the nerve to ask her to dance but her brush-off is instant and total "Get lost, creep!" she says. Complete humiliation.

As Dick and his business associates remain indoors obsessively discussing collateral, loans and interest rates, his wife and her new pal stroll the seafront, with Diane Keaton looking the part of a college girl on vacation: floppy hat, T-shirt, denim shorts, kneesocks and sandals. Then Dick fixes him a date with Julie, a girl from his office, but in a bar two giant bikers hijack Julie and beat him up.

Later, back in town, Linda is being totally neglected by her husband and loves the little plastic skunk Alan has given her for her birthday. She enjoys him more and more and sees a lot of him between visits to her analyst three times a week. One day in the park they realize they are falling in love. They plan an evening together at his place, dinner and watching the late movie which is *The Big Sleep.* He says he has frozen steak and a bottle of champagne, and she plans to buy some vegetables and come round and cook for them. He is thrilled.

"You can open the champagne" she says, "But not if I'm the only one who is going to drink it."

"No," he cries, buzzing with anticipation. "I'll have one or two but you have to promise to put me to bed if I dance naked."

Waiting for her to turn up, his mind is full of new anxieties. She arrives. In a kitchen scene, while discussing an Ida Lupino movie, she asks the Big Question:

"Do you think it's possible to love two people at once?"

He fumbles, stumbles and hesitates.

"Go ahead, make your move," urges Bogie, appearing now to advise at this dramatic juncture. "Go ahead, take her and kiss her. Go ahead, she wants it."

He is paralyzed.

"Well, kid, you blew it."

"I can't do it. How does it look? I invite her over, then come on like a sex degenerate? What am I, a rapist?"

As tension builds, Dick phones. Alan is by now imagining himself on the front page of the National Enquirer, a tabloid rag devoted to the exploitation of lurid crimes. Then, on the sofa with Bogie coaching him line by line, phrase by phrase, he tells her she is beautiful and has irresistible eyes.

*Casting a critical eye
over the rushes of Annie Hall*

Linda: Alan, your hand is trembling.

Bogart: That's 'cos you're near, tell her.

Alan: That's because you're near.

Linda: You really know what to say, don't you?

Bogart: Tell her you've met a lotta dames but she is really something special.

Alan: That she won't believe.

Bogart: Tell her!

Alan: I've met a lot of dames but you are really something special.

Linda: Really?

Alan: She bought it!

As he puts his arm round her, he knocks a tablelamp which falls off and smashes. They struggle and argue. It's a farce. She exits. As he imagines a visit from the vice squad, she comes back in the door.

"Alan, Alan, did you say you loved me?"

She kisses him passionately. Romantic piano melody, an instrumental version of *As Time Goes By.* Cut to bed scene, morning.

Then she says they can't sneak around and have an affair, it would be cheap. They wonder which one of them should tell Dick, who is out of town, and agree that she should. Walking around the streets of San Francisco, Alan is deliriously happy. For a change, he is high on himself: "Well, kid, she loves you. And why not? I was dynamite in bed last night. Lucky girl! I gave her my best moves." His mood is euphoric. In an antique shop he meets Nancy his ex-wife, and plays it cool. He rationalizes Linda's adultery, and his betrayal of his best friend. His mood continues to be self-congratulatory: "Linda finds me exciting. What the hell, Dick'll understand. Because of our social encounters, a little romance has developed. It's a very natural thing among sophisticated people."

Still strolling the streets on an "upper", he is surprised to bump into Dick who unburdens himself to Alan about his fear that Linda is having an affair.

"The other night she spoke about having an affair in her sleep."

"Did she mention any names?"

"Only yours. I woke her and questioned her and she said it was just a nightmare."

Back at home alone Alan is very worried in case she has told Dick. He phones her four times but she is with Dick and keeps hanging up, saying she will talk to him later. His mind is running amok. He gets a taxi to the airport. He confers with his fantasy alter-ego again.

"Its got to end and I don't know how to do it."

*Sweet serenade for Diane Keaton in Play It Again Sam.*

"It's not that hard," says the maestro of tough talk. "Watch."
He proceeds to give an exhibition of the hardest of hard-boiled dialogue.
This is how to talk to dames:
"Come here sweetheart."
"Yes, darling."
"It's over."
"What is?"
"Us."
"Over?"
"Thats right, toots. Over. Kaput."
She pulls a shooter.
"Now come off it, sugar, you never could use a rod."
He slaps her and takes the gun.
"But why does it have to end before it can begin?" she asks.

Bogie's tone of voice is aggressive, dismissive and heavily sarcastic.
"Because you play too rough for me, sugar. It was you that killed Johnson, and Parker found out about it so you killed him too but that wasn't good enough for you, you wanted to finish me off too, you knew you couldn't do it while I was facing you so you figured you could get me to turn my back. But not me, sugar, Now let's go. You're taking the fall."
"Yer, but being tough with broads is easy for someone who's Bogart."
"Everybody is, kid, at certain times."
Bogie tells his protégé he's passing up 'a real tomato' but there's other things in life besides dames; one of them is knowing you did the right thing for a pal. At the airport, as fog swirls round the runways, Alan finds Linda, and they decide to call it quits, to the strains of *As Time Goes By,* one of the most romantic songs ever written.

Whatever films, plays and books may still be waiting to be unlocked from his fertile imagination, *Play It Again, Sam* will remain the definitive image of Woody Allen's public persona. Not because it's the only time he's introduced us to Woody the nervous, inept and luckless lover, but because it's the time we recognize him most clearly, the only time we can identify with him instead of just looking on.

For more than one generation of movie freaks, Bogart symbolizes the man who is *comfortable* around women, the guy with the self-assurance and the guts to be tough with them. He doesn't need to put on a macho mask — he only needs to be himself. When Woody enlists the support of Bogie's spirit, he's only doing what most of men try to do from time to time, perhaps a little less consciously.

*'Play it again Sham',*
*Allen as Bogart as Allen.*
*'Ingrid Bergman' looks on*

# Elegant Slapstick in 2173

With *Sleeper,* Woody took another major step. It was a classy comedy in the tradition of Chaplin and Keaton with a sophisticated plot, intricate sets, and a risky dependence on special effects and complicated machinery. It went beyond anything he had attempted before.
Ralph Rosenblum.

A man, Miles, goes into hospital with an ulcer and instead of having a minor operation accidentally gets involved in a space-time experiment.
He wakes up in 2173, after the holocaust in which almost all of our civilization has been destroyed. All that's left is a Playboy centerfold, some news photographs and a fragment of film of Richard Nixon. In the fascist utopia which now exists the masses are passive, sedated by TV and orgasm-machines. A dictatorship rules using secret police, liquidations and brain laundromats. The ideal woman of the future is played by Diane Keaton. She goes crazy when deprived of her opiates, degenerating into a howling imbecile.
Although there is the usual verbal satire, the movie is extremely visual: sight gags, slapstick and chases predominate. In a series of hilarious set-

pieces, self-contained comic episodes, he borrows gags from the great silent clowns. From Buster Keaton's *The Navigator* he lifts the device of an inflated spacesuit which turns Miles into a canoe. From Harry Langdon he borrows the baby gestures suitable to his emergence into a new world. Like Harold Lloyd he runs up and down the outside of buildings, using computer tape. Woody's improvement as a physical comedian is considerable here; he uses his body better than ever before. Disguised as a robot, he resembles Chaplin when threatened by a giant mechanic who wants to replace his head.

*Sleeper* was a success with the critics. One London critic rated it the finest comedy of the year. He was amazed that Woody was able to draw on so many sources of comedy and still make a film which was all his own. "He is as original as any of the great silents: the ultimate urban weed and color supplement intellectual, with his pallid, anguished face haloed in wispy red hair; his large appalled eyes behind the hornrims, his convinced cowardice and his unconvinced assertion of ever-ready virility."

It was only Woody's fourth film as director, but The New Yorker's formidable Pauline Kael rated it a small classic, the most stable and sustained of all his films. She considered it a triumph in certain important aspects: "To have found a clean visual style for a modern slapstick comedy in color is a major victory: Woody Allen learns with the speed of a wizard. *Sleeper* has a real look to it, and simple, elegant design."

The concensus verdict was that the film was smooth, controlled and more strictly cinematic than his untidy early efforts. He had perhaps been impressed by the fluency of Herb Ross's direction on *Play It Again, Sam,* and decided to make this one more sober, less deranged, with no rough edges. Ralph Rosenblum agrees that it was clearly his best so far. "*Bananas* was a better film than *Take The Money* but it was still unstructured and frenetic without much refinement of plot. With *Sleeper* Woody took another major step. It was a classy comedy in the tradition of Chaplin and Keaton with a sophisticated plot, intricate sets, and a risky dependence on special effects and complicated machinery. It went beyond anything he had attempted before."

The film was planned as United Artists Christmas release. Budgeted at $2 million and allowing 50 days for filming, it began shooting on April 30th 1973. When Rosenblum arrived in California in August, Woody was already some weeks into 51 days of additional shooting, which had already consumed the $350,000 fee he was due as actor, director and co-author of the screenplay. Longtime associate Jack Grossberg, who had brought the

editor in originally to rescue *Take The Money,* was worried that the release date was in jeopardy.

As Rosenblum says "the deadline could only be broken at serious cost to
the company, the director, and the relationship between the two."

The pressure of this situation exaggerated a conflict between Woody and
Jack, who parted company at this point. While shooting was still in pro-
gress, Ralph began editing at Woody's HQ, a cottage which had once been
Clark Gable's dressing room. Working seven days a week with a local
editor and two assistants, he finished a rough assembly of most of the movie which they took back to New York.

Then, each working separately on different segments with an assistant,
Ralph and Woody cut it down to two hours and twenty minutes by the end
of September. By mid-October they had it down to 100 minutes. Woody
then went to New Orleans to record the score, playing clarinet with the
Preservation Hall Jazz Band. In mid-November Rosenblum again objec-
ted to the ending: "To redo it, Woody returned to California for a Sunday
shooting about two weeks before the picture was released. Diane Keaton,
by then working on *The Godfather,* had to switch back into her role as the
light-headed Luna on her day off. It was only through a whirlwind of over-
lapping labor that we made the Christmas release."

In this period Pauline Kael has argued that Woody did not really give himself other characters to respond to. Reviewing *Sleeper* she said "so far in
his movies he's the only character, because his conception of himself
keeps him alone. When we see his films, all our emotions attach to him: his
fear and his frailty are what everything else revolves round. No-one else
in his films has a vivid presence."

Perhaps, she wonders, he does not invest other parts with comic character
because he is so hung up that he has no interest in other people's hang-
ups. Her main complaint, as we've seen, is that Woody is here less crazy,
less messy, less liable to let his disruptive inspiration run wild. The film is
stylish but too sober, and the end is mild, unexciting because the routines

*On turning 40:*

*I dated a 21 year old. Took her to my apartment.*
*Put on a record of Charlie Parker and Dizzie*
*Gillespie playing a Cole Porter tune.*
*She thought it was classical music.*

don't accelerate, gather momentum and finish with a bang. "Woody Allen loses his supporting players along the way and one hardly notices. It's likely that he sees his function as being all of us, and since he's all of us, no-one else can be anything."

Her summary is sensible, perhaps the best. "If it sounds like a contradiction to say that *Sleeper* is a small classic and yet not exhilarating — well, I can't completely explain that. Comedy is impossibly mysterious; *Sleeper* is a beautiful little piece of work — it shows a development of skills in our finest comedy-maker — and yet it's mild, and doesn't quite take off."

# From Russia with love and death

Sonja: Sex without love is an empty experience.
Boris: Yes, but as empty experiences go, it's one of the best.

In a Russian jail in 1812, Boris is waiting for the firing squad. As he waits, he reminisces about his past life with his father, mother, two brothers, and, most vividly, he recalls how he was madly in love with Sonja, his beautiful cousin, while she only had eyes for his hulking brother Ivan.

The three brothers go off to war when Napoleon invades Austria and threatens Russia in 1805, with cowardly Boris far less eager for battle than Ivan and Mikhail. Before they go, Ivan announces that he is going to marry Anna, which causes Sonja, in a fit of pique, to decide to marry Voskovec, the herring merchant.

There are boot camp scenes which are somewhat similar to the military training antics in *Bananas,* as Boris gets trained to be a soldier. He learns that the lovely Sonja is miserable with Voskovec, and is taking lovers; when Voskovec dies she goes to the battlefield and becomes a nurse on the frontline. In a fluke bout of combat Boris kills some French officers, is wounded, and of course, taken to the hospital where he meets Sonja again. Suddenly a war hero, he returns triumphant to St Petersburg where he has

77

his pick of the ladies. He spends a frantic night with the alluring Countess Alexandrovna (played by brunette bombshell Olga Georges-Picot) and is then challenged to a duel by her lover, Anton. Convinced the duel will be his last, Boris begs Sonja to become his wife and since she also feels sure he will be killed, she marries him, and then when he is only wounded (in a farcical spoof of dueling ritual where he walks towards his adversary, not away) she is stuck with him. At first the marriage is a fiasco, but the pair gradually grow to love each other.

When Napoleon invades Russia in 1812, she decides they should go to Moscow to assassinate him. On their way to the capital they are accompanied by their serf, the village idiot, who is going to Minsk, where he is attending a convention of village idiots. Several other idiots are mucking about in the mud when they drop him off outside an inn, beneath a huge banner proclaiming 'Welcome Idiots'.

Gavin Millar noted that Woody had become a master of timing. From the idiots he immediately whisks us on to the next joke before we have time to realize they have no relevance to the plot. "After several films Woody Allen as a director and not only as a performer, has become an expert in screen comedy timing. The very last shot shows him dancing away from us down an avenue of trees in the company of the Grim Reaper. It lasts well over a minute — well beyond, in other words, any normal expectation. The effect is to remind us that the joke is serious. If *Love And Death* is better than any of Allen's films to date, it is partly because, for all its hysterical fun, it seems to be in deadly earnest. The title points to his obsessions."

On the road they stay in the same hotel as Don Francisco of Spain and his sister who are also on their way to see Napoleon. So Boris and Sonja swap places with them and Sonja lures Napoleon to her room but Boris can't bring himself to kill the Emperor because he's "probably someone's grandfather." So their assassination plot collapses, she escapes, he is captured and condemned to death.

In his cell he has a vision of an "Angel of God" who says he will be reprieved at the last minute, but Boris is somewhat dubious: "Yea, though I walk through the Valley of the Shadow of Death — or on second thoughts, even better, though I run through the Valley of the Shadow of Death — that way I'll get out of it quicker."

Sure he will not die, Boris refuses the blindfold and cockily asks the firing squad to stand nearer so they will not miss. They don't miss. He is executed. Later, when Sonja sees him being led away by the Grim Reaper she asks what it's like to be dead. "It's bad" he says. "How bad?" she wants to know, and he replies "You know the chicken at Treskey's restaurant? It's worse."

Woody told Charles Marowitz for a 1977 article in the *New Yorker* that his first three films were trivial and purely for fun. "They were absolutely for fun. *Sleeper* is slightly more satirical, but has a slight point — nothing profound, but a slight point about the way I thought society was moving. And *Love And Death* also has a slight satirical point about dying and war, and the transitory quality of love. But again, not profound at all, just a minor little theme.

"As soon as you start to want to say something meaningful in comedy, you have to give up some of the comedy in some way. You have got to be willing to go more in the direction of writers like, say Mark Twain or Salinger or Philip Roth or Saul Bellow — people like that who can be quite funny and satirical, but what gives the substance to their work is a willingness to be unfunny a certain amount of the time."

These days the screen comedian is concerned with an interior psychological world, whereas the great silent clowns were involved with the physical world. In *The General,* it was the world of the train; in *The Navigator,* it was the world of the boat, or the athletic Harold Lloyd hanging from buildings. Today, as Woody says: "What really concerns people are the motivations and the subtleties of psychological anxiety and neurosis, and these are not subjects for the traditional cinematic comedian."

Asked by Charles Marowitz about Woody's appeal and influences Pauline Kael said: "I would say the clear influences on Woody, and he acknowledges this himself, are performers such as Bob Hope. I do not particularly like *Love And Death* and I don't particularly like the Bob Hope movies it resembles, which are the Bob Hope movies of the Fifties, but the character is very similar: when Bob Hope played those coward-heroes, those ones we found amusing because they were always running from danger and always being menaced, he was an amusing eccentric. When Woody does it, it's a response to the whole macho mood of our time, so he stands for the whole generation that was anti-Vietnam, he stands for all the people who are anti-macho."

Marowitz comments that "despite the darker implications of the later films, Allen has not been able to merge the density of the subject matter with a consistent comedy tone. If one wanted to push this criticism even further one could say that most of his films are really a series of short takes: a hammock of splendid gags, slung between two flimsy bits of bamboo."

Logistically, the epic scale of *Love And Death* proved to be something of an ordeal. It was shot mostly in Hungary with assistance of the Russian Army, and needed many extras and special effects experts flown in from London. Woody found Budapest freezing and windy, and in breaks between filming took refuge in a more comfortable base in Paris. Here, unhappily, he was hounded by the French press, and pursued by the relentless *paparazzi,* whose popping flashbulbs even followed his party into restaurants.

According to Rosenblum, *Love And Death* is the climax of Woody's love affair with esoteric humor. "It was something that was always apparent in his other films. In *Bananas* a baby carriage flies out of control down the steps of the capital as the rebels take the city. The dictator, seeking American aid, misses the CIA offices and walks into the UJA offices instead. In *Sleeper* someone tells the wakened Woody two hundred years after he was put into frozen suspension that World War III was started when someone named Albert Shanker got hold of the atom bomb. How many viewers knew that the baby carriage is a reference to Potemkin? That UJA stands for United Jewish Appeal? That Albert Shanker is the aggressive and much publicized president of the New York teachers' union? These jokes are like a special reward for people who share Woody's background and tastes. *Love And Death* is brimming with esoteric references, mostly to Russian literature, and because of my love for the originals, it is one of my favorite Allen films."

He also reveals that Woody had originally planned to use the music of Stravinsky in the film, but it was found to be too dramatic. Overpowering. At Rosenblum's suggestion, they used three compositions by Prokofiev, one of the editor's best-loved composers. This gave Rosenblum a special thrill. "It was a heartwarming moment for me, the first time I sat through the screen credits and saw 'Score by S. Prokofiev', in part because of my fondness for the composer, but more because of my fondness for the director and the freedom he has given me to contribute to his work."

Certain references in Woody's films are so esoteric that only about three people in the world understand them. One such concerns Vicky Tiel, a girl who, as a teenage art student, used to pass the hat for up-and-coming folkies like Richie Havens and Bob Dylan in the good old days at the Cafe Wha, the Figaro and other nurseries of the acoustic music scene in Greenwich Village. When she was 20 she went to Paris to get a job as a designer's assistant, but wound up doing costumes for *What's New Pussycat?,* and dating Woody and Clive Donner.

"I wasn't sleeping with either of them," says Vicky, "but the crew decided

that whoever gave me the best birthday present could have me." So Clive gave her a gigantic box of chocolates from Lady Godiva and Woody gave her a pinball machine, and the film crew decided she had to spend the following night with Woody, who instructed her to come to his hotel suite, strip off in the bathroom, and join him in bed. At lunch in the canteen that day she met Ron Berkeley, who was Liz Taylor's make-up man, fell in love at first sight, spent the night with him, stayed with him for seven years, married him, and is still married to him.

Today when she goes to see Woody at his apartment he shows her his collection of porcelain. "Look at all the china we could have had!" he says. In *Manhattan,* Diane Keaton's dog is called Wuffles after Vicky's dog, and the line where he says to Tracy "You can't leave me, you can't go to Europe, you might go out to lunch" refers to her traumatic non-appearance at Woody's hotel.

# Annie Hall romps to four Oscars

For all its apparent frankness there's something re-assuringly old-fashioned about *Annie Hall.* Romance lives, even if these days you have to punctuate it with visits to the shrink.
Joan Goodman, Time Out.

Alvy Singer is doing a monologue to camera. "Annie and I broke up" he says, and goes into a lot of rapid chatter about his Brooklyn childhood. We flash back to him as a bespectacled kid.

"He's stopped doing his homework," shrieks Ma, panicking.

"What's the point?" says the precocious Alvy.

This is the notorious world of the over-protective, over-achieving Jewish mother, from which have sprung millions of jokes like "Help, help — come quick, my son the lawyer is drowning." We learn that as a kid Alvy got his aggression out in bumper cars (Dad has the concession) but has difficulty distinguishing between fantasy and reality. In a grainy, discolored TV clip we see comedian Alvy/Woody as a guest on the super-hip Dick Cavett show.

Then comes the sequence about the intrusive fan. Woody, pathologically shy, loathes being approached by strangers. This scene shows just what an embarrassing nuisance the pushy fan can be. In a street scene, Alvy is

HUMPHREY BOGAR
Across the Pacific
MARY
ASTOR
SYDNEY
GREENSTREET
Directed by
JOHN HUSTON
Presented by
WARNER BROS.

waiting outside a film theater and is recognized by an obnoxious male pedestrian.

"You're on the Johnny Carson show, right?"

Alvy looks beautifully exasperated.

"Once in a while," he admits. The guy then goes wild, yelling things like "Dis guy's on television!!!" and "Kineye 'ave your ortograph?"

Just then, in a brilliant establishing moment for a new character, Diane Keaton arrives in a cab, gets out and snaps "I'm in a bad mood, OK?" She has come to meet her date and the first thing she says is not "Hi!" or "Hello, darling" or "Sorry I'm late" or anything, but "I'm in a bad mood, OK?" Wonderful! A perfect moment!

As they stand in line, waiting to see Bergman's *Face To Face,* she explains how she is depressed through missing her therapy because she overslept. The man in the line behind them is opinionating loudly about a Fellini movie. They try to ignore him. Alvy is getting very annoyed. Annie indicates that she does not want a scene. "He's spitting on my neck!" says Alvy. The obnoxious phoney then starts pontificating about Canadian media guru Marshall McLuhan. Alvy goes over and triumphantly produces, from behind a screen, the real Professor McLuhan who tells the startled phoney: "You know NOTHING of my work!"

Annie and Alvy are in love. They whiz merrily around in her VW. She is deliciously attractive and charming in her baggy pants, black waistcoat, white shirt and black tie with spots, but she is also gauche a hick who thinks that some of Sylvia Plath's poems are "neat".

Always a poet of Awkward Scenes With Girls, Woody constructs another memorable one around Annie And Alvy as they begin to get acquainted. In a balcony scene, with a funky ramshackle cityscape in the background, the pair have a hilarious exploratory conversation. The scene has an amusing Dick Lesterish use of subtitles. As they exchange banal smalltalk and minor compliments, what they are really thinking appears in bubbles above their heads, things like (above Annie's head): "He probably thinks I'm a yo-yo." The thought-bubbles are quick, clever and funny, although this kind of witty device is not one which a director can use very often, or it rapidly becomes a tiresome gimmick.

There are bedroom scenes where Alvy leaps under the sheets in his shorts and socks, and bookstore scenes where he buys her a lot of books about death. Once, after they have made love, he declines a joint. He disapproves of her smoking dope.

"Grass, the illusion that it makes a white woman more like Billie Holiday."

"It relaxes me," she says, negligently.

He insists that getting a laugh from people who are stoned doesn't count, because they will laugh at anything. This is true, although few will dare to suggest it. She loves his cleverness. In a park scene he makes fun of various members of the public who are out of earshot. Annie giggles, and moves in with him. He tries to insist that she keeps her own apartment, even offering to pay the $400 a month rent.

This part of the film contains one of the classic pieces of Woody Allen verbal humor. Annie is thinking aloud. "Sometimes I wonder how I would stand up against torture," she muses. Alvy says "The Gestapo would take away your Bloomingdales charge card and you'd tell them everything." A great joke, a definitive joke: witty, gentle, mildly chauvinist and anti-bourgeois.

Alvy does a stand-up comedy spot for a college audience. He meets her

*Playing clarinet at Michael's Pub in New York City.*

parents and in an aside to the camera, says "Nothing like my family." We cut to a flashback to a room full of noisy, crazy, competitively babbling Jewish neurotics. At dinner he is so paranoid that he has a flash, imagining that they see him as an old bearded Hassidic rabbi.

Later, she confesses that she's having an affair with David, her college professor, and complains that Alvy will never take her seriously "because you don't think I'm smart enough." Then later when he is in bed with a skinny reporter from Rolling Stone (Shelley Duvall) Annie phones him at 3am. It's an emergency. He rushes over to her apartment. There is a spider in her bathroom.

"Be careful!" she pleads.

"Darling, I've been killing spiders since I was 30."

He goes in, bravely. Then she hears his voice say "Honey, there's a spider in your bathroom the size of a Buick."

He sorts out the problem. She cries. "I miss you," she says. They go to bed. "Alvy, lets never break up again." Then she falls for a smoothie LA rock tycoon Tony Lacey (Paul Simon) and goes to live with him in California, Alvy flies out to try to win her back. The mood of the film is light, fast and jolly. The problem areas of their relationship are exploited for their comic potential: her family, her use of soft drugs, her affair with tacky Tony. These scenes are played for laughs, not drama. Reviewing the film when it opened the 1977 Edinburgh Film Festival Jan Dawson wrote that it "continues Allen's running reflection on the human condition as compounded in equal parts of sex, death and the movies. It's full of self-mocking homages to Allen's favorite film-maker, Ingmar Bergman." Although superficially poles apart because of a difference in tone, she reckons "Allen's underlying philosophy is not that far removed from the gloomy Swede's. His funniest gags are all rooted in desperation, in turn provoked by the lack of a deity, by the transience of human relationships in general, and by his inability to keep a girlfriend in particular."

Much of what has been written about *Annie Hall* has been puzzling. Consider the following comment by Ralph Rosenblum. "It was a story told with great wit and humor, which generated more laughter than any previous Allen film, and with a denouement which left many viewers in tears."

Tears?

It was a fun film. A light, playful, painless film. A nice little romantic comedy. It is odd to think that *Annie Hall* could have moved anyone to tears. It does not seem the kind of film that would engage the emotions in that way. *On The Waterfront* engaged the emotions. *Chinatown* made you care whether or not Faye Dunaway was killed at the end. *Manhattan* made you want Tracy to come back from London when she was 19 and carry on the story. But *Annie Hall?* Surely not. It was a romp, *Butch Cassidy* without horses. Superior light entertainment, an abundantly accessible, charming romance.

In fact, it was never intended to be a love story. *Annie Hall* was not written or filmed as a movie about the Keaton-Allen relationship. Throughout 1976 Woody had wanted to gamble on something different, and planned a film called Anhedonia, a psychological term meaning the inability to experience pleasure.

Co-author Marshall Brickman is quoted by Ralph Rosenblum in the latter's *When The Shooting Stops:* "The first draft was a story of a guy who lived in New York and was forty years old and was examining his life. His life consisted of several strands. One was a relationship with a young woman, another was a concern with the banality of the life we all lead, and a third was an obsession with proving himself and testing himself to find out what kind of character he had."

Remember, the film as we know it is a 94-minute comedy-romance. In the autumn of 1976, it was something else. Rosenblum recalls "The first cut of what has come to be known as *Annie Hall* was two hours and twenty minutes long and took us about six weeks to complete. Far from being the story of a love affair... it was the surrealistic and abstract adventures of a neurotic Jewish comedian who was reliving his highly flawed life and in the process satirizing much of our culture." As always it was short of narrative, and Diane Keaton made only one brief appearance in the first 15 minutes. Amid a mass of material, enough for two or three films, Woody dwelt on many issues: his envy of athletes, his obsession with proving himself; his distaste for intellectuals. "The movie was like a visual monologue, a more sophisticated and more philosophical version of *Take The Money And Run.* Its stream of consciousness continuity, rambling commentary and bizarre gags completely obscured the skeletal plot."

This we can easily believe. But isn't it where we came in, way back in 1968? The key phrase here is "visual monologue". In a film which is essentially episodic, where one thing leads to another because it precedes it, you can have continuity without story, but that kind of continuity depends on one performer being on the screen all the time. You can wind up with what is too obviously a comedian's film about a comedian.

Marshall Brickman was devastatingly disappointed when he saw the first rough assembly. He felt the first 25 minutes were a disaster, and that the film did not get going until Paul Simon appeared. "It was a very commentative film — and Woody of course is brilliant at that — and it was funny, but, I felt, non-dramatic and ultimately uninteresting, a kind of cerebral exercise. Stuff that's wonderful fun to write is often less fun for the audience to see and that stuff that Woody and I had written was cerebral, surreal, highly intellectual, overliterate, overeducated self-conscious commentary. And just for a moment I had a sense of panic; we will be humiliated, is there any way to stop the project?"

Still working on a film about a jaded comic who can feel no joy, they began cutting in favor of the present-tense material, compressing the opening

*The Oscar - winning Annie Hall*

monologue to six minutes, and establishing Diane Keaton more quickly. As the film moved more and more towards her, they trimmed other relationships (his first wife Alison is dealt with in a 4½-minute flashback, his second wife Robin in less than three minutes), dropped a lot of the academic one-liners and kept Annie and Alvy together onscreen together for long periods. Woody admits "It was originally a picture about me, my life, my thoughts, my ideas, my background, and the relationship was one major part of it."

As a package, it now had wide appeal. Previous films had been cults because they were about a zany little guy with glasses. With a big role for a glamorous comedienne, *Annie Hall* now had potential as mass entertainment. The photogenic Diane Keaton was a bonus and the clothes — the Annie Hall Look — were a godsend for feature space in newspapers and magazines. As a comedy it was refreshing, appealing and accessible. Its key elements were the raw material for a big marketing campaign which became ANNIE HALL: A NERVOUS ROMANCE.

How autobiographical was it?

Diane Keaton's real name is Diane Hall, and she used to live with Woody in real life, so people have insisted on believing that most of the film is true. Not so. "Very little of the film is autobiographical," says Woody. "I was playing myself, but not in autobiographical situations for the most part. There were a couple of things there that were based on reality, but I was not born underneath a roller coaster on Coney Island, nor was my first wife politically active, nor was my second wife a member of the literary set, nor did Diane leave me for a rock star or to live in California."

One incident which was based on real life was where Woody-Alvy meets Diane-Annie's family for the first time. "It was the quintessential kind of Gentile family. I was very conscious of my Jewishness when I met them originally, over Christmas dinner. They were very different from my own family. And there is a Granny Hall — that was Keaton's grandmother. She always had a dim view of Jews, as moneylenders and people who usurp all the good jobs and start wars and things."

Diane Keaton told Time Out's Joan Goodman that she thought the film was more than a trivial middle-class entertainment. "I think one of the reasons the film has done well in the States is that a lot of people feel the same way. Some people have come up to me and said, there's so much of what we feel in it. It's about relationships now, and what it's like for us. I mean, obviously there's been a change. There's many more people who are single and not actually ready to get married at later ages. Woman who are 30 and not ready and not knowing if they want to get married and who are still finding out about themselves."

"I don't see myself as a Woody Allen actress. I don't think that's my role in life. But then, you know, it's been great being in his movies. I have difficulty in expressing myself — obviously — and I'm a clown in some ways. It's a behavior thing. I've known Woody for eight years now and he listens to me and that's a great thing for me. Prior to Woody I didn't really have an opportunity to say what I thought a lot. With him, I don't have to worry if this person's going to like me, because I know Woody's going to like me. I feel very comfortable with him."

Woody's view of his role in the movie business is not geared to maximizing grosses. "I have a nice gentleman's agreement with United Artists. I've traded the idea of making millions in return for artistic control. My films have a very modest audience — they don't make anything like a Streisand or Redford picture. But I make them very cheaply and they produce a small

*"Well, lah di dah!"*
*Boy meets Girl in Annie Hall*

profit. As long as that goes on, UA is happy. They leave me alone and I deliver them a finished movie."

He said this before he really knew how big *Annie Hall* was going to be. In April 1978, at its annual ceremony in Hollywood, the movie industry conferred four of its five grandest prizes on Woody's film. *Annie Hall* took four Oscars: Best Picture, Best Director, Best Writer, and to Diane Keaton, Best Actress. Since he has never had much time for the brilliant throng of thronging brilliance in the movie capital, Woody did not attend, preferring instead to play his clarinet as usual in Michael's Pub that Monday night. He did not compromise his convictions merely because he was likely to win. Despite also being voted Director Of The Year by the New York Critics, and in the BAFTA Awards, Woody still feels more comfortable as a writer. "Writing is more fun than anything else, because nothing can go wrong that can hurt you, if you're just locked in at home," he told the BBC's Iain Johnstone. "If you have problems, no one will ever know. But if problems develop while you're filming or editing or in any phase when you're actually in contact with other people, it's not too pleasant. I've never made a film in my life that I've really liked. You get a real good feeling when you think of an idea for a movie. You're home alone, and it's perfect. You see it in your mind's eye and everything jells. Then you write it, and it's not so hot because you had realistic problems. Then you film it, and it gets a little worse. By the time you've cut it and the film comes out, its about 50 or 60 per cent of what you had conceived of. So it's always a big let-down."

"I know it sounds horrible but winning that Oscar for *Annie Hall* didn't mean anything to me," he told Marc Didden in 1979. "I have no regard for that kind of ceremony. I just don't think they know what they're doing. When you see who wins those things — or who doesn't win them — you can see how meaningless this Oscar thing is. It has nothing to do with artistic merit. It's a sort of popularity test. When it's your turn, you win it."

The Oscars were, though, national recognition for the back-up team behind Woody. His producers Charles Joffe and Jack Rollins have been partners for more than twenty years. Active in management as well as production, their speciality over the years has been in creative talents at the 'highbrow' end of showbiz. As well as Woody Allen they have handled some of the cleverest and funniest people in the entertainment industry, names like Mike Nichols, Elaine May, Dick Cavett and Louise Lasser, as well as singers like Harry Belafonte.

Brooklyn-born producer-manager Charles Joffe handles most of Woody's affairs and has power of attorney to sign all his contracts, even his divorce

*The young stand - up comic*
*'doing a Gene Kelly' in Paris.*

papers. His "deal" is said to be less lucrative than it might be because Woody rarely sells him films to network television, and because he would rather sacrifice cash than give up the complete creative control he enjoys. Individually, both Rollins and Joffe have both been TV producers. Rollins was the executive producer of The Dick Cavett Show, while Joffe produced two Woody Allen Specials, one for CBS and another for ABC. Joffe also produced *Everything You Always Wanted To Know About Sex, Take The Money And Run, Love And Death,* and was executive producer of *Play It Again, Sam, Bananas, Sleeper* and *The Front.*

Rollins and Joffe co-produced *Manhattan* and *Annie Hall,* receiving Oscars for the latter in 1978.

# Interior decorating

By this stage of his career Woody has presumably achieved what he always yearned for. Colossal success and recognition as a comedy actor-writer-director. But this was obviously not enough.

He wanted to be more than a comic. In an interview with Gene Sistel he explained. "My feeling is that in comedy you don't deal with the issues directly. You're always deflating them. You're always distancing yourself from them. Whereas with tragedy you come dead square and confront the issue and work it through." As a moviegoer he had always professed to have preferred "heavy dramatic fare" as he mentioned after his involvement with the *The Front.*

"I enjoy sitting through serious films and getting a long, slow workout. I see Bergman's films over and over again. There are always those *superb* moments. Brilliance falls off Bergman like perspiration."

His increasing directorial ambition displayed in both *Love and Death* and *Sleeper* probably made it inevitable that Woody would seek a shift away from taking a central action rôle in his films, and similarly, the encroaching elements of psycho-drama in *Annie Hall* hinted at a shift away from comedy. The result was *Interiors.*

"I was fully prepared to be ridiculed. I knew there was a good chance I would make a terrific fool of myself. I was very nervous on that first day of rehearsal, very apprehensive about my bad writing. It's one thing to send a script to actors and *imagine* how they sound reading your wonderful lines for the first time, but when you actually hear those lines being read aloud, it's like taking a cold shower."

Such artistic insecurity apart, in financial terms, the potential loss of credibility with investors could also have sent palpitations through the Brooklyn boy's body. However, as Geraldine Page, one of his leading ladies explained:

"Every film director I've worked with would like to have the kind of resource Allen has earned by making profits for his investors. His demands were great, his discipline rigid, his sights well set, but the fluidity of the situation inspired rather than stifled creativity."

It is a drama of lugubrious intensity, a story of family life and emotional deprivation, in which there is desperation, but not laughing desperation. There are no lobsters stuck behind the stove and no little guys in glasses saying to shrieking women. "Talk to him! You speak shellfish!"

Allen announces his intentions firmly from the opening frame. After the starkly simple black and white opening titles, the first shots are of an empty room, Chinese vases, and the shadowed faces of people gazing enigmatically out of windows at the sea.

Like Bergman's *Autumn Sonata,* it concerns a mother who is artistic, fastidious and impossibly overbearing. Eve's home is like a museum, swathed in unrelenting tones of beige and grey, it exerts a chilling hold over its occupants. She manipulates her family's feelings, ensnaring each of her children in a web of guilt and dissolving their independance. She is an emotional dictator made vulnerable by her own extremism.

Her children likewise, for all their earnest self-analysis, are unable to help themselves. Her three daughters are Renata, a blocked poet whose novelist husband Frederick resents her greater success and vents his rage in vicious reviews of contemporaries; Flyn, the least cerebral, is an actress in trashy west coast movies; and Joey, married to radical film-maker, Mike, the quiet, frustrated youngest one who keeps switching jobs, can't face either herself or motherhood, and is closest of the three to her parents.

As the film starts, the father, Arthur, announces over the breakfast table that he wishes to spend his remaining years with a woman he has just met on vacation.

He is moving out right away. The daughters say that this will kill mother. Sure enough, in a characteristically thorough operation, Eve, not able to

*Buttonholed by fans*

endure the prospect of isolation, attempts to gas herself. Broken and incapable of objectivity she deludes herself that the status quo will be restored and her husband returned. Her children bearing the marks of her personality are unable to respond.

Meanwhile, Arthur is seeking a final divorce settlement. He introduces his new companion, Pearl, to the girls over dinner. She is a warm, boisterous, spontaneous figure in a red dress. Pearl provides an explosion of color and candor that ricochetes through the chill, arid order that Eve had created. Pearl likes food, music and dancing and dares to suggest redecoration.

Eventually, one stormy night, finally shattered by some home truths from a drunken Joey, Eve walks out into the seething Atlantic Ocean and kills herself.

The next day, the day of the funeral, the sun shines for the first time. The three daughters, have at last found some sort of unity through their mother's death and the film ends with their profiles facing the sea and the future.

In a T V parody Allen once wrote of *Wild Strawberries* that there's a credit: 'Written, directed, produced and understood only by Ingmar Bergman'. Despite this the final sequence is undeniably Bergmanesque bearing close comparison with the closing shots of *Persona;* two characters frozen in profile, symbolizing a conjoining of spirit.

Many people saw in the ending for the three women only the bleak prospect of the duplication of their mother's problems, but as Allen said, "... I saw the ending in a more positive way, I felt there was hope for the sisters, that they had arrived finally at a point where they could communicate."

Indeed the whole film prompted a great discrepancy of opinion. Frank Gaguard found it "sterile, secondhand, self-conscious and self-parodying", whereas for Alexander Walker "*Interiors* is the work of an artist whose potential we thought had been fully and satisfyingly realized in other kinds of film; with this one Woody Allen gives us the enormous excitment of seeing gifts in use that we never suspected he possessed. It is not too soon to anticipate myself and declare *Interiors* the film of the year." A little overboard maybe. Certainly one can point towards an over-explicitness of intention. Perhaps in his desire to wear a straight face after *Annie Hall* he over-reacted to his task — his characters are so unremittingly humorless that they lose credibility because of it, making the 'vulgarian' Pearl more welcome than she ought to be. The one-liners need not dry up completely. Indeed Bergman uses them to stunning effect, punctuating the most grisly of serious situations.

Allen pursues the theme of thwarted creativity and the emotional mentor evolved in *Play It Again Sam* and developed further in *Annie Hall.* In *Annie Hall* it was the hypocritical Alvie who tried to organize Annie's life when all she wanted to do was sing. In her dreams she saw him as Frank Sinatra with glasses trying to smother her with a pillow!

In *Interiors* it is Eve, the paragon of refinement who soars over her children like a marble Venus. She herself had her artistic ambition, but her promise was stunted by the proximity of her husband and her rôle as mother. Likewise both Renata and Joey have permutations of the same problems in their marriages; when their mother has been dispossessed it is these two and Flyn who adopt the mantle of emotional steamroller as they deal harshly with their father's choice in Pearl.

Dramatically, and thematically, it is with our response to Renata and Joey that the essential stumbling block to the movie presents itself. Involvement with them is crucially hindered by the fact that the family background is not elaborated in enough detail to let us judge for ourselves the validity of, for examples, Renata's claim that Joey feels guilty for rebuffing her mother, or Joey's that Renata is wary of her as a competitive threat. Allen's delineation of those literary-artistic lives is more damaging still. They really do verge uncomfortably close to unwitting parody. When Renata continuously attempts to convince her husband of his talent as a novelist, or declares that she is preoccupied with death but "the intimacy of it embarrasses me"; or when Joey voices a "need to express myself, but I don't know what I want to express," we seem to be only a hot dog's length away from the bogus cineaste in the movie line in *Annie Hall.*

What links these characters is an obsession with a way of living rather than living itself. "There always was a kind of harmony," says Arthur, "but it was like an ice palace." Likewise Joey fears being "swallowed up in some anonymous lifestyle." These implications are never worked through despite the aid of the blanket beige and grey tones surrounding all characters. Except Pearl, dressed in life-blood red. In fact the device is so obtrusive it highlights the stylistic uncertainty.

*Interiors* has also been criticized for being too self-consciously an attempt at Art. Film with a capital F. Some have tilted at "painstakingly aesthetic camera angles" and "glowing Bergmanesque images." Not Philip Bergson, however.

"Spare, chamber-cinema, shot through a lens in close-ups and scenelets, it unnervingly evoked Bergman — perhaps more in parody than homage, for I suspect that underneath it is an exquisite jest, though in earnest the sort you smile at with tears in your eyes."

The last words must go to Woody. In an interview with Marc Didden he was asked if he consciously tried to 'do a Bergman'.

"*Interiors* is a story that came to me in different parts. Some characters came to me years ago, some parts of the story too, but none of it materialized. As a matter of fact I have always wanted to make serious films — in addition to comic films — and when I got the opportunity and I felt the time was right, *Interiors* happened to be the first one that I made. I would like to think that it was successful enough so I can make more of them, which wouldn't mean that I would just have to make amusing films. I simply think that I have enough ideas in my head to make a serious film now and then. I was not trying to prove anything. And when I say 'serious' I only mean a film that is not primarily intended to make the audience laugh.

"If I have somehow succeeded in making *Interiors* a decent movie it is because I have some knowledge of theatrical construction. I'm very conservative in my view on story-telling. Films without a story and a good construction are often very boring films. Certain masters like Fellini and Bergman can, of course, break the rules. They can make films without obvious construction. But I don't have that kind of confidence in my talent. I feel I could make a funny film without any plot in it and I could invent enough funny things to make sure the audience enjoys the film but I surely do not have that skill for serious work.

"I am not from now on trying to make any Ingmar Bergman films. Bergman can take care of that. I really don't think I should ever have said in interviews how much I admire Bergman. If *Interiors* has to be compared to something I really think it's closer to bad O'Neil, bad Chekhov or bad Strindberg than bad Bergman. Conflicts between people, in life and in movies, used to be much more physical than they are now — Chaplin, Buster Keaton used to hit each other over the head all the time, fall over, lose their trousers all the time. Now characters talk about what's going on in their minds.

"Conflicts happen inside people, which makes it hard for a film-maker to show what's going on in their minds. Bergman developed a personal, visual vocabulary to do that. When Bergman photographs somebody's face for two minutes, for some reason it's not boring Everybody is fascinated. I would not dream of doing that. That's one of the reasons I don't like being compared to Bergman, although it doesn't really bother me. A critic that doesn't see a difference between my film and Bergman's is just not sensitive enough to be allowed to talk about movies."

# Maturity with Manhattan

For me there were two important films in 1979. Woody Allen's *Manhattan* was one because it is intelligent without betraying the real nature of the cinema, which is to be entertaining. *Manhattan* is almost unique among American films in Europe since it is never melodramatic, banal or tedious. My other favorite was *Don Giovanni* by Joseph Losey.
Lilliana Cavani, Italian director.

*Manhattan* is Woody on his own turf, where he is unassailable. He is doing here what no one else can do: satirizing that strata of chic metropolitan life where everyone works in media or showbiz, where everyone has an analyst, and where everyone (but everyone!) is writing a book, or thinking about writing a book.
The film is a comedy-drama about how love in the big city is affected by neurosis, fear, friendship and time. And about how a pretty woman is bad news if she can't handle being intelligent and single. The pretty woman is Mary, a smarty-ass journalist who can't deal with the lifestyle of a bright single woman in New York. She thinks she can, but she can't. Everything about her is a mess, except her jackets: she has the greatest collection of stylish, well-tailored jackets ever seen on any woman in any film. Men fall

for her. She arrives in the story and breaks up two beautiful relationships. The characters all know each other when the films begins, except Mary. This familiarity allows maximum conversation and a lot of intimate characterization. It's a kind of equation: familiarity = rapport = energy = reality. Bob Dylan once referred to this in an interview. Talking to *Playboy* about a scene with Joan Baez in *Renaldo And Clara* he said "Seems pretty real. Just like a Bergman movie, those things seem real. There's a lot of spontaneity that goes on. Usually the people in his films know each other, so they can interrelate. There's life and breath in every frame because everyone knew each other."

Woody has romanticized New York, obviously. What is interesting is that he has romanticized it in such a clever way. He has made a film which is both modern and old-fashioned. By the stylized use of music and Gordon Willis's black and white photography he has given it an aura of nostalgia which is how he wants to express the character of his hero Isaac Davis who is writing a book about the city he loves, and whose voice-over starts the film:

"He adored New York City..."

We hear him writing and re-writing the introduction to his book. The visuals are a montage of street scenes and skylines, fancy shops and restaurants, a road-mending crew, a floodlit baseball stadium with an elevated train snaking along in front of it...

"New York was his town, and it always would be."

Then we see four friends sitting round a table in a crowded restaurant-bar. They are Yale (Michael Murphy) and his wife (Ann Byrne) and Isaac (Woody) and Tracy, played by Mariel Hemingway, the youngest of Ernest Hemingway's three granddaughters; sister Joan is a novelist and glamorous model Margaux is now also an actress who appeared with Mariel in *Lipstick*.

Isaac, drunk but coherent, reveals that one of his ex-wives, who left him for another woman, is writing a book about their life together. It's agreed that this is a pretty tacky thing for her to do. "Gossip is the new pornography," says Yale. After dinner they take a leisurely stroll home, with the two females trailing behind, walking and talking some ten or twelve yards behind the two men. Yale confesses to Isaac that he has met a very nervous, highly-strung lady journalist and is having an affair with her.

"I hate myself when I'm doing it," he says.

The next scene is photographically brilliant in the way it introduces another character to the story. We see the glacial blonde Jill (Meryl Streep) come out of a building. The camera follows her as she swans swiftly, majestically along the pavement, with Isaac fluttering and scampering alongside, protesting and begging her not to crucify him in her book. Jill has regal presence and looks the epitome of the immaculately independent New Woman, while he buzzes below her like an annoying insect. She refuses even to break stride to give him the time of day. In a flawless tracking shot the meaning of one of the most arresting scenes in the whole film is expressed with brilliant economy. The dialogue just adds detail.

In a cozy scene at home with Tracy he tells her "When I was your age I was being tucked in by my grandparents." At an art gallery they bump into Yale who introduces them to Mary, who turns out to be extremely tiresome, an opinion-machine forever rattling off her pretentiously provocative views on this and that. Clever, but ignorant. She and Yale mock Mahler and F. Scott Fitzgerald in their "Academy of the Overrated."

Then Isaac quits his job as a comedy writer on a television show. In a short brilliant scene confined to the gallery of the TV show where they are taping the program, Isaac paces up and down, as if in a cell, and starts a tirade. He can't write this crap any more, he slanders the show and bawls out his zombied workmates for taking 'ludes, downers: "You should abandon the show — and open a pharmaceutical house!" His rage is visceral, and this scene is possibly the angriest and most decisive scene Woody has ever allowed himself onscreen.

Isaac talks over his decision with Yale who congratulates him and says now he can concentrate on his book. But Isaac is worried because his stocks are down, he has two alimonies, he'll have to move to a cheaper apartment, and he'll have to give his parents less money, which his father won't like. "He'll have to sit at the back of the synagogue — away from God!" The subjects of Woody's jokes have not changed much in fifteen years, as we are reminded at a black-tie charity event starring Bella Abzug. Among the usual cocktail chatter a sad blonde remarks "I finally had an orgasm, and my doctor told me it was the wrong kind."

Romantic scenes alternate with satirical ones. Orchestrated George Gershwin music escorts Isaac and Mary as they walk her dachshund. She talks incessantly about herself. She married her teacher at college. "I was sleeping with him and he had the nerve to give me an F!" They walk by the river. "My book is about decaying values," says Isaac. The pair are so tuned in to each other by now, they sit on a bench by the river and talk till dawn.

Being a gentleman, Isaac phones up his buddy to ask how hung up Yale is on her. Answer: very. We see Yale and Mary together in Bloomingdale's with her saying "I don't want to break up a marriage" and the infatuated Yale swooning over her like a lovesick puppy.

Isaac visits his kid Willie who lives with Jill and her lesbian partner. Jill asks a favor. "Can you take Willie for the weekend of the 16th? Connie and I are thinking of going to Barbados." This is fabulous dialogue because it contains a lifestyle in a line. This is a world where women can afford to go to the Carribean *for a weekend.* Woody has a genius for the remark which encapsulates a whole way of life. They argue about the intimacies to be disclosed in the book.

"I'm not gonna dwell on the part where you tried to run her over," says Jill. Isaac persistently denies this accusation. It was dark, it was raining, he didn't see Connie, he insists.

Mary phones Yale one Sunday afternoon but he can't get away from Emily to meet her as planned, so she calls Issac who is delighted to oblige, since he is only passing the time reading the lingerie ads in The New York Times. They get caught in a thunderstorm in Central Park, take refuge, dripping, in the Museum Of Modern Art, and talk about her. "You rely too much on your brain," he says. They whisper their way round the spooky lunar landscape of the planetarium. "You think I have no feelings, right?" she says. Back with his young girlfriend, he finds that Tracy, a drama student, has been offered a chance to study at the Academy of Music And Dramatic Arts in London.

"So go!"

"So what happens to us?" she says, complaining that he won't take her seriously because she's seventeen. They go for a horse-drawn buggy ride, cuddling and necking affectionately.

Meanwhile Yale and Mary are at each other's throats, or, rather, she is at her own throat, chastising herself for having an affair with a married man. Her self-analyzing, self-lacerating spiel is punctuated by the phone ringing and the dog barking. Fast, nervy chatter spurts from her like a burst water pipe. Yale stands there slobbering and whimpering as she says "I'm beautiful, I'm bright and I deserve better!"

In his new, cheaper apartment Isaac leaps around complaining about night and neighbor noises. Brown water runs from his taps and he complains about it now and later, again and again. A running gag. Tracy still wants to know "What's gonna happen with us?" Over lunch, Yale tells Mary he thinks they should stop seeing each other. "I knew it would end this way and now its happened I'm upset," she says, dashing round to Isaac's to

106

take half a valium.

In the next Tracy & Isaac-at-home scene, they are watching TV in bed, guzzling late night snacks out of cartons and talking about how they hate aging actresses who have facelifts because they are too vain to grow old gracefully.

During a squash game Isaac and Yale talk about Mary. Or rather, they discuss her on a squash court while vaguely waving their racquets about. "Call her up! She likes you," says Yale, fraternally. "I think you guys would be good together!" Next, before you can say Shohei Imamura, the new couple are seen coming out of a Japanese art movie. Back at Mary's place, he kisses her. No furniture is wrecked. Bogart does not appear. She says she thought he wanted to kiss her that day at the planetarium and Isaac says he would never do a thing like that to his buddy Yale. He is a moralist who would never kiss his best friend's mistress. She continues on her favorite subject: "I'm not the person to get involved with, I'm trouble." He talks about his failed marriages. "My first wife was a kindergarten teacher, then she got into drugs and moved to San Francisco. She went to est, became a Moonie. She works for the William Morris Agency now." The screenwriter who can put a lifestyle into a line here compresses a decade into four lines. Woody Allen, famed for his one-liners, should get credit for writing brilliant three-liners and four-liners as well.

Unfortunately, his worst, silliest preoccupations and habits still get the better of him occasionally, as in the next scene. Mary sits on his lap. Fair enough. She says "What are you thinking?" Also fair enough; all women say this. Then he blacks out the lights and the screen totally for Isaac's reply: "I'm thinking there must be something wrong with me because I've never had a relationship with a woman which lasted longer than Hitler's with Eva Braun." This is a clumsy, pretty meaningless line. It is NOT funny, and it is a pity to find Woody, after ten films, still guilty of such foolish moments.

In a drugstore/soda shop were they meet after her classes, Isaac tells Tracy that he has decided to dump her. When he says "I don't think we should see each other any more," she is confused.

"I'm not hung up on you, I'm in love with you," she says.

"The truth is that I love somebody else," he says.

She is devastated, and starts to cry.

"I can't believe you met somebody that you like better than me."

He does not tell her who it is.

On what seems to be a weekend away in the country, the new lovers are in a relaxed, playful mood, enjoying each other. Bed talk still tends towards the analytical and critical, with behavior being monitored far too much. She laughs when he suggests she was faking it just a little when she bit his neck.

"I feel good around you," she declares.

"I don't blame you! he replies, wittily triumphant. She even suggests that Isaac is someone she could imagine having children with. Later, a romantic rowing scene on a lake is a cue for the film's first sight gag. When Isaac trails his hand in the water, it emerges covered in black filth.

He goes to look at a new car with Yale and Emily, who quizzes him.

"We never see you these days."

"I'm working so hard on my book."

"It's that girl, when are we gonna get a chance to meet her?"

As two couples they attend a classical concert with Mary sitting between the two men, of course. Moments of slight awkwardness. On a shopping trip Isaac and Mary bump into her ex-husband Jeremiah who turns out to be short, bald and nondescript. After the way she had previously described him as some splendid, magnificent animal, Isaac is underwhelmed and mystified. Almost to himself he says "I guess all that stuff is so subjective..." The surprise of the ex-husband's appearance is another sight gag. Jeremiah is played by Wallace Shawn, a playwright (whose *Marie And Bruce* is a savage comedy about Manhattan manners).

At home we see Isaac reading in one room and Mary typing in another.

"Why are you wasting your time on a novelization?" he asks.

"'Cos its easy and it pays well."

When Yale buys the new Porsche sports car he has lusted for, the four of them drive across bridges with their hair blowing in the wind. Some of the imagery in the film is hackneyed, to say the least. At the beach the foursome see Jill's book 'Divorce Marriage And Selfhood' in a shop, buy a copy and walk along the pier. Isaac fumes and cringes as excerpts are read aloud. Needless to say, it is highly unlikely that they would discover the book in this way. Woody sometimes tries a little too hard to make use of outdoor locations.

When Isaac has the How Could You? confrontation with Jill she is unrepentant and zaps him with the possibility of further indignity: "I better warn you, I've had some interest in the book for a movie sale." Worse is soon to come, for Mary then drops her bombshell:

"I think I'm still in love with Yale."

He is speechless, almost.

"Jesus, I'm shocked."

"He wants to move out of his place so we can live together."

"What does your analyst think about this?"

"Donny's in a coma, he had a very bad acid experience."

Has Mary driven her shrink to drugs? Or is she an idiot for going to a doctor who is an acidhead?

Next comes one of the key serious scenes in the film, with Yale and Isaac. They argue but the argument is not really about Mary but about the way people should live. Isaac lectures his friend who accuses him of wanting to be God. "You're too easy on yourself," Isaac says. "It's very important to have some kind of personal integrity." This is Woody the moralist. It's hard to be a saint in the city, but you've got to try.

Alone and introspective on his sofa at home Isaac dictates into a cassette recorder a list of things that make life worth living:

Groucho Marx.

Willie Mays.

The second movement of Mozart's "Jupiter" Symphony.

Louis Armstrong's "Potato Head Blues."

Flaubert's "A Sentimental Education."

Tracy's face.

He gets up slowly and goes to find the harmonica she gave him earlier in the film. He stands holding it for a long moment. Then he moves to the phone, changes his mind, goes outside and starts to run down the street, very realistically. Not for him the bionic sprint which got Dustin Hoffman to the church on time in *The Graduate,* and would have worried Sebastian Coe.

He runs urgently, for many blocks, slowing and puffing and stopping once to phone from a callbox, but the line's engaged. He runs on. As the music reaches a crescendo, he arrives at her apartment building. A doorman is loading her suitcases for the trip to London. Tracy, looking more adult, is standing in the foyer brushing her hair. She sees him through the glass door. Silently her face is required to convey surprise, anger, affection, exasperation. A serious, poignant scene like this is particularly difficult to write and direct at the end of a film because it has to say "Why?" and "Please Stay" and "I love you" and "Goodbye" without being corny, and it has to find a good line or gesture to end on.

The scene is all dialogue. The pair do not touch or kiss or embrace at all during a conversation which is tender, honest and beautifully exact. He says he wants her to stay, she asks if he still loves her and he says yes, she says six months isn't such a long time and he says he doesn't want the thing he liked about her to change. The lines are perfect, and what's left unsaid is great, too. The conversation is so good, it defies summary. Woody gives the girl the last line: "You should have a little faith in people." Shot of skyscraper skyline: THE END.

What of the people in *Manhattan?* What can we say about the behavior of the main characters? What can we learn from the liaisons of chic folks whose cleverness extends only to the endlessly narcissistic examination and re-examination of their own moods and motives? Are they, as Isaac says about people in *Manhattan* in a story he is dictating, "constantly creating these real unnecessary neurotic problems for themselves that keep them from dealing with more terrifying unsolvable problems about the universe?"

Isaac is a jerk because he abandons a good girl in favor of a silly one, preferring adult neurosis to uncorrupted innocence. He can't see what he has, although Tracy can: "We have laughs together. I care about you. Your concerns are my concerns. We have great sex." Mary is a mess, and Yale is a jerk because he would rather have a Porsche than the baby his wife expects from him after 12 years of marriage. Emily and Tracy are the most sympathetic, and have the most sense. Jill is looking out for No. 1. Maybe the message of the film is that we should let relationships run their course. The chemistry of mutual human attraction is mysterious and can easily bridge the gap between a teenage student and an adult writer, even if he is older than her father. Certain pairs work, simple as that.

At the time one wondered about Woody's move into black and white. To take color off the screen is to leave the cameraman working exclusively with tones, shapes, faces and movement, and many directors enjoy this. Billy Wilder hates color. Fellini adores black and white, especially black: no one does more with black than the mad Italian, whose weakest film, *Casanova,* was in color.

In *Annie Hall,* color helped to make the film highly accessible, and Woody probably did not want to be accused of making Annie Hall II, another eye-catching entertainment which would be instant, guaranteed box-office. Formula. Perhaps he did not want it to be tagged as a Sensitive Little Comedy like *Girlfriends* or *The Goodbye Girl.* Both of these warm little films would be OK if you took color out of them, but somehow if you put color into *Manhattan* you would cheapen it. Lack of color has an effect on the way we perceive characters. It makes what they wear less important and what they say more important. Maybe, it seemed at the time, it was too

soon after Mazursky's *An Unmarried Woman,* another New York film in which Michael Murphy leaves his wife.

Woody's own explanation of the move was straightforward. In *New Musical Express* Marc Didden asked him why *Manhattan* was in black and white. "Because that's how I remember it from when I was small." he said. "Maybe it's a reminiscence from old photographs, films, books and all that. But that's how I remember New York. I always heard the Gershwin music with it, too. In *Manhattan* I really think that we — that's me and cinematographer Gordon Willis — succeeded in showing the city. When you see it there on that big screen it's really decadent. Black and white is beautiful, that's evident. When a woman dressed in black and white enters a room she has a strong chance of being tagged 'elegant'. Part of its beauty in movies is, of course, that it's rarely used."

He also talked about his leading lady. "Diane Keaton is a limitless actress. If you're doing a heavy movie, a musical, a funny movie, no matter what it is she can do it and do it very well. So I like the idea of always working with her. Also, because she's a close friend of mine and one of the very few people whose advice I take seriously. She even chooses the titles of some movies I've made. I wanted to call *Interiors* something like Night Visions. She hated it, she thought it was too heavy, too Bergmanesque. And she suggested *Interiors* which is indeed a much better title. You might say I rely on her to a degree. If she thinks a script is no good I might very seriously not make the film. Also, working with people you know so well really saves you a lot of time while you work."

"I'm not sure I like Diane so much, though, in other people's films. I can't say I like *Looking For Mr Goodbar.* But then again she was brilliant in *The Godfather.* But it pleases me that sometimes she's very good in very bad movies. She always makes the director look good. I honestly think she's the best American film actress. People will say I'm prejudiced when I say that, but I'm not. I said this before anyone ever knew her."

Gavin Millar, reporting from the Cannes Festival, loved the ending, and the film. "It feels like a masterpiece. What he nearly caught in *Annie Hall* and went over the top with in *Interiors,* he has finally hit fair square and unwaveringly. The difficulty has been to bend his own wryly self-deprecating, wise-cracking personality away from farce and towards serious drama without losing the jokes: not exactly a tragic clown, but at any rate a funny and intelligent man in whose life small tragedies reasonably occur — lost loves, fuddled careers, missed opportunities.

"The film ends with the resigned, amused, doubting gaze he turns on Tracy

*Looking chic in Paris.*

as she leaves, confidently, for the airport. In its comic perplexity and depth of feeling, funny and poignant at the same time, it finally puts Woody up with Buster Keaton, where he belongs."

Most critics, like Millar, feel *Manhattan* is his most mature and definitive film so far. In a cover story in Time, Frank Rich said it was the movie *Annie Hall* hinted at, a film which never ceases to be funny but starts to be something more. "Isaac Davis is the central character, and the mainspring of a masterpiece is that perfect blending of style and substance, humor and humanity that his friends and followers were convinced he would one day make. It was also a rare summarizing statement, at once assured and vulnerable, in which an artist casts a selective eye over the fantastical life of his times and shapes his observations into an unsparing, compassionate, always, witty and radically moral narrative. Tightly constructed, clearly focused intellectually, it is a prismatic portrait of a time and place that may be studied decades hence to see what kind of people we were."

Under the headline WOODY PUTS IT TOGETHER — AT LAST another top British critic, Alexander Walker of the London Evening Standard, declared it a film both romantic and tough and Allen a "Jewish genius who has no equal when it comes to capturing the spirit of his times in the home of his choice."

The concensus view was that Woody had managed to become funnier and more serious, at the same time. As Walker noted "Its gags are more part and parcel of its bag of seriousness than they were in *Annie Hall.* Its pessimism is lightened with more dazzling satire than it was in Allen's last ultra-solemn film, *Interiors.* This is the whole wry sandwich of human frailties that Woody Allen can't live without consuming — or digest without suffering heartburn. It lasts just under 100 minutes but you have to keep your ears strained like radar cups. So precisely nuanced is the speech, so subtle the behaviour of a group of friends, lovers, mistresses and cuckolds who keep splitting up and pairing of like unstable molecules."

Time Out editor John Fordham met Woody at the posh Plaza Athenee hotel in Paris in April 1979, under the chandeliers of the giant dining room, where several giants were having lunch. Actually, it is a *cavernous* dining room. "Such an establishment is pretty much exposed territory for a man who makes so much of a joke out of being overwhelmed by contingency, and Woody Allen appropriately enters in a darting, sidelong fashion, like a man backing along a parapet. He wears a sports jacket and pullover, brown cords and check socks, as if the only natty part of his attire had to be kept well out of the limelight. Later he is to meet Simone de Beauvoir for tea in his suite. It is a full day."

Woody lamented the decline of the apprenticeship for comedians. In the Fifties the great training ground for comedy was a string of Jewish-run holiday hotels in upstate New York where comics could do a series of one-night stands known affectionately as the Borscht Circuit. Most good comedians started there. Mel Brooks met Sid Caesar there when he was a drummer and Sid was a saxaphone player.

"There's nowhere for the young guys to learn how to do it any more, and be able to trust what they learn. In the theaters, where that was where you mostly worked, you just had to get the laughs. Chaplin, Keaton, the Marx Brothers, they all started out having to get the laughs. On television nowadays you don't have to do that because they put the laughs on afterwards, so you can't know what the reaction to your material really is."

"It's true of course that people still recognize good stuff, which is why all those old people are still popular, and good stuff does keep coming to the surface. It's just that there is so much junk around that it gets more difficult to tell good from bad, in *anything.*"

"I think with *Manhattan,* that I've integrated things more, and let the story speak for itself. It's like a mixture of what I was trying to do with *Annie Hall* and *Interiors.* In *Interiors* I deliberately restricted myself from using any jokes at all, trying to concentrate on the people and why things go wrong for them. In *Annie Hall* I was still looking for the laughs. I think *Manhattan* has a balance that lets the laughs come out of the action more."

In interviews with Woody certain ideas and phrases keep cropping up. Two words he uses a lot are "decent" and "junk". He told Frank Rich that *Manhattan* deals with the problem of trying to live a decent life amidst all the junk of contemporary culture, — the temptations, the seductions. So how do you keep from selling out?

"At the personal level, I try to pay attention to the moral side of issues as they arise and try not to make a wrong choice. For instance I've always had a strong feeling about drugs. I don't think it's right to try to buy your way out of life's painful side by using drugs. I'm also against the concept of short marriages, and regard my own marriages [five years to Harlene Rosen, two years to actress Louise Lasser] as a sign of failure of some sort. Of course I sell out as much as anyone — insidiously. It's impossible not to be a sellout unless you give away all your physical possessions and live like a hermit."

During the making of *Manhattan,* he spent dozens of hours watching Bob Hope movies to compile a one-hour film tribute for a gala honoring the

comedian at the Lincoln Center. "I had more pleasure looking at Hope's films than making any film I've ever made. I think he's just a great, huge talent. Part of what I like about him is that flippant Californian, obsessed with golf, striding through life. His not caring about the serious side at all. That's very seductive to me. I would feel fine making a picture like *Sleeper* tomorrow, but I get the feeling the audience would be disappointed. They expect something else from me now." He admitted regretting having had to cut some jokes out of *Manhattan.* "They were very funny — not just one-liners, but sight gags — but in the context of the film, they looked like they had dropped down from the moon."

Talking about his next film, he said he hoped it would go deeper in both the comic and the serious directions. "I want to make a film that is stylized and very offbeat. I want to try being funny without jokes, to rely less on dialogue and try to tell the story in images more."

The new film has already been the subject of a lot of gossip in New York. In the Voice there is a hip column called 'Bell Tells' in which Arthur Bell feeds fans with a lot of inside info from the world of the arts and entertainment. Last December he wrote: "For nearly two months now, Woody's been shooting WAFP, short for Woody Allen's Fall Project (*Manhattan,* for a while, was WASP — it filmed in the spring). Already WAFP is five weeks behind in a 22-week shooting schedule. It's about a filmmaker surveying his own life: the script is cluttered with flashbacks, stream-of-consciousness, and all sorts of digressions. Woody's aiming for Fellini's *8½* with a touch of Sturges's *Sullivan's Travels.* Some of it is depressing. The character played by Philip Anglim dies. Tony Roberts acts himself, and Judith Christ plays herself. Off-Broadway types such as as Judith Cohen and Helen Hanft are featured (Hanft's got a juicy part), though the movie, as reported elsewhere, stars Charlotte Rampling, Marie-Christine Barrault, Jessica Harper, Daniel Stern and Amy Wright. Gordon Willis is photographing in black and white, just as he did in *Manhattan.*"

117

*'Tracy' and 'Isaac' make*
*music together in Manhattan*

# Writing about writing about writing

> Wisdom is hard to find. Happiness takes research. The message that large numbers of people are getting from *Manhattan* and *Interiors* and *Annie Hall* is that this kind of emotional shopping around is the proper business of life's better students, that adolescence can now extend to middle age.
> Joan Didion, 1979

Although she is a novelist and screenwriter, Joan Didion is best known for her two collections of New Journalism, 'Slouching Towards Bethlehem', and 'The White Album'. The title essay of the first book is a long, stylish and perceptive piece which makes taking drugs sound as dumb as anything I have ever read. In 'The White Album' one essay describes the torture she endured during a crass promotional tour for her novel 'A Book Of Common Prayer'.

Didion also has considerable credentials as a film critic. Interestingly, in 1964, when she was film critic for Vogue, Didion was years ahead of her time in her judgement of the genius of Billy Wilder. Every critic except Didion slammed *Kiss Me Stupid,* in which a hooker fantasizes playing a wife for a day and a wife fantasizes playing a slut. In a brilliant satire on the sleaziness of America, the immigrant from Vienna put Kim Novak in a story which featured Dean Martin playing himself. Where everyone else found the film offensive, squalid and tasteless, Didion (to her everlasting credit) was tuned in to the disillusioned romanticism which informed Wilder's unique and daring vision. Though not one of his classic comedies, *Kiss Me Stupid* did not deserve to be buried as smut.

There again, a critic who chooses the right moment to say the exact opposite of what other critics are saying can often attract a disproportionate amount of attention. The timing of her anti-Woody piece was nothing if not opportunistic.

Because she disagreed, she was news. Again.

First published in the New York Review Of Books, her now notorious essay was printed under the headline 'The Self As A Career'. In this she lambasts the notion of the self as something to work on, and work at. She attacks the characters in the three films because they are with one exception presented as adults whose concerns and conversations are those of clever children.

"Self-absorption is general, as is self-doubt," began Miss Didion. "In the large coastal cities of the United States this summer many people wanted to be dressed in 'real linen' cut by Calvin Klein to wrinkle, which implies real money. In the large coastal cities of the United States this summer many people wanted to be served the perfect vegetable terrine. It was a summer in which only have-nots wanted a cigarette or a vodka-and-tonic or a charcoal-broiled steak."

She then itemizes Isaac's list of reasons for staying alive. "This list of Woody Allen's is the ultimate consumer report, and the extent to which it has been quoted approvingly suggests a new class in America, a subworld of people rigid with apprehension that they will die wearing the wrong sneaker, naming the wrong symphony, preferring Madame Bovary."

Didion makes her key blunder early in the essay, in criticizing Woody's audience. "The people who go to see these pictures, who analyze them and write about them and argue the deeper implications in their texts and subtexts, seem to agree that the world onscreen pretty much mirrors the world as they know it."

This is arrogant nonsense. How can she presume to know whether his fans are all living in the same world as Isaac and Alvy? Are they all comedians and comedy writers? This makes as much sense as saying that 'Soap' fans tune in to see the world pretty much as they know it. She ignores the fact that two of the films are comedies and one is a drama. Many of the millions who adored *Annie Hall* probably never saw *Interiors.* They are very differ-

*Shades of romance beneath*
*Brooklyn Bridge in Manhattan*

ent films with different subjects, and each appeals to a separate audience. And of course Didion and her writer husband, John Gregory Dunne, are no less self-absorbed than the rest of us. She is always going on about her migraine, he is always on about his stutter. While she whines about having to endure idiot interviewers in order to become rich, he re-lives his nightmare of writing and rewriting the script of *A Star is Born* for Barbra Streisand. Oh, the horror! The horror!

She chooses to ignore Woody's satirical intelligence, and underrates his fans who clearly do not go to his films expecting to see the world as they know it, but to escape into the smart, entertaining worlds of the witty little New Yorker they have come to know and love. Further, it is misguided to assume that Woody approves of the behavior of the main characters in *Manhattan.* He obviously disapproves of the two men, and of the Diane Keaton character (Mary) while admiring the young, loving, forgiving girlfriend (Tracy) and the older, loving, forgiving wife of his friend (Emily). More than in any previous film, he's making judgements about a group of characters, but he's also laughing at them, and asking us to laugh at them. If he has a weakness it is the same weakness as J.D. Salinger, who was himself once a cult hero of the college audience. Salinger used to write stories for people who could read without moving their lips and now twenty years later Woody Allen, the livewire auteur of the audio-visual age, is filming stories for people who can watch TV without moving their lips. Tracy and Isaac are not Franny and Zooey on celluloid, but Allen and Salinger are perhaps both guilty of loving their characters too much: the concern for the nuances and convolutions of the individual psyche is immense, perhaps excessive.

In the Village Voice, America's first (and still best) radical newspaper, Andrew Sarris knew which side he was on in this debate. He knew that a backlash was inevitable. "It started with Joan Didion's diatribe against *Manhattan* in The New York Review Of Books. Like the rest of us Didion has had her ups and downs as a polemicist, and it was hardly to be expected that she would look with favor on a professional New Yorker who did everything but defecate on her beloved California ethos in *Annie Hall.* More questionable was her refusal to recognize Allen as an evolving artist from picture to picture."

Sarris has the sanity to see that Didion's interpretation is utterly unfair. "By lumping together his gags from many movies, she created the impression that his movies are interchangeable, whereas for many *Manhattan* represented a spectacular stylistic advance."

For anyone with eyes, *Manhattan* was a spectacular stylistic advance. Sarris continues: "Also, Allen started turning some of the jokes against himself, and the resultant parody produced the climactic egg-on-his-face ending that is in its way worthy of comparison with Chaplin's final close-up in City Lights. Certainly Allen never *acted* so brilliantly and so subtly as he did in *Manhattan.*"

He notes that the sexual humor and comic vision of Jewish novelist Philip Roth was not effectively translated into film in *Goodbye Columbus* or in *Portnoy's Complaint,* whereas Woody has control and knows how to transfer his ironic sensibility intact to the screen. "This feat of unalloyed auterism from a New York base cannot have endeared Allen to the California-commited Didion with her sacramental interpretation of the Big Deal as the secret of movie-making. Not that Allen's detractors all live near Big Sur. He has enemies enough in New York, particularly now that he has actually transcended New York. For me *Manhattan* remains a monument of cosmopolitan grandeur in the contemporary cinema."

In his piece "The New Phase Of Intelligence" (Voice December 3rd, 1979) Sarris says there had been no great thematic or stylistic breakthroughs in films anywhere in the world in the last decade, and that cinema is tending more towards consolidation than innovation. "When people asked me what the difference was between old movies and new movies, I replied that in the old days stupid people made stupid movies, whereas now intelligent people made stupid movies. Hence, contemporary stupid movies are more corrupt and perverted than the ancient models. Young people, in particular, seemed to delight in 'selling out' as soon as possible. Through the 70s I felt that American movies were regressing to the point that anyone over 14 years of age would eventually be excluded from the taste-making process. In this context 1979 has been a very pleasant surprise for grown-up movie-goers. It is not a full-fledged renaissance to be sure, but for the first time there are signs of a sustained sophistication in movie-making."

As a pro reviewer, Sarris sits under an avalanche of garbage. It is his job to watch bad films, and he sees more of them than any film-goer. So he's extra grateful for any screen entertainment which does not insult his intelligence. In an earlier piece he had cited six films in this category: *Head Over Heels, "10", Manhattan, North Dallas Forty, Starting Over,* and *Breaking Away.* "What pleases me particularly about *Manhattan* and *"10"* is that intelligence not only exists in American cinema, but that it is currently very profitable, which means that American audiences are more

*Surrounded by admirers at Michael's Pub - all jazz buffs for the evening.*

intelligent than the new bottom line moguls have given them credit for being."

In Britain, too, there has been a backlash. Suddenly, Woody Allen became
ultra-fashionable. As his popularity reached higher than ever before, it
reached the point where it began to work against him.

Decadologists were calling him a Seventies phenomenon. He was rated
up alongside disco, jogging and punk, and as such he was fair game. We
build them up, and we knock them down.

Woody was the target of a hatchet-job in one of England's better Sunday
papers, The Observer. In a long editorial feature which was part of the Observer's Review Of The Decade, he was fingered by Peter Conrad as part
of the problem, not part of the solution. The tone of this piece was evident
from its marathon headline which ran across sixteen columns and two

center pages: AN INERT, NUMINOUS STUPOR WAS THE MENTAL CON-DITION OF THE DECADE... INFANTILE, NARCISSISTIC... EVEN SEX, THAT BOLD INVENTION OF THE SIXTIES, IS NOW IN RETREAT.

The article argued persuasively and provocatively that in the last ten years we have all grown backwards, that nihilistic punks were right to spit on the Seventies, that Californians live in a state of anesthetized bliss, and that the mood of the decade was nostalgia, which "conveniently trivializes the past by unlearning its lessons and promoting its junk to the status of art." In one marvellous, gloriously glib paragraph he reminds us how Jack Nicholson started out as a boisterous rebel in *Easy Rider* and ended up with a lobotomy in *One Flew Over The Cuckoo's Nest.* Anyone who can write comments as entertainingly facile as that is a bad sociologist but an ace typewriter-jockey, and just the man to hire when you want someone to gallop through ten years of cultural history in 2000 words. Mr Conrad continues: "The idols of our narcissism are figures like the pumped up Arnold Schwarzenegger, immured within an armory of tumescent muscle, the jiving John Travolta, or even Woody Allen, whose satiric pretence of self-disgust masks a consuming self-love. Wrinkling his gnomic phiz he grimaces at his teenage girfiend in *Manhattan,* unable to comprehend her refusal to share his self-adoration. Allen stooped and balding perpetual adolescent has become a totem for our times, and no wonder. The nympholepsy which incites him to pound after Mariel Hemingway is another symptom of the contemporary jogger's disease. This wizened dwarf is actually in love with the remote recollection of his own youth, for the Seventies is the decade in which those who were young in the Sixties began to creak, limp and wrinkle."

Of course Woody Allen is in love with himself. So what? All creative people are. Of course his anxieties and neuroses and self-loathings are a pose. Of course he thinks he's talented. If he was really as worried about things as he pretends to be, he would never even leave his apartment, let alone tell jokes to thousands of strangers, or spend millions of dollars turning his daydreams into celluloid.

Allen is a little guy who has the misfortune to be born skinny and short-sighted. Luckily, he was bright, and not scared of hard work, so he sweated and struggled and invented a personality for himself and created material to amplify that personality into comic characters on the screen, and in time, although he was still a weedy bespectacled runt, he became a successful entertainer and a star.

Mr Conrad does Woody the colossal disservice of misrepresenting his finest work of art for the sake of one newspaper article. A journalist sharp enough to realize that "*Apocalypse Now* is the last and deadliest insult preferred by the Seventies to the Sixties" should have been smart enough, if he wanted to slag off Woody Allen, to attack the over-rated *Annie Hall*. Instead he frisbees his own credibility out the window by choosing to attack the wrong film at the wrong moment for the wrong reasons.

Times have changed, anyway. They may not have changed for the better, but they have changed, and it's no longer unusual for men to have young girlfriends. Back in 1955 when middle-aged Humbert Humbert moteled round America with the precocious Lolita, all hell broke loose. Pornography! they screamed, although in Time the book was recognized as a major novel by one of the most sophisticated fiction writers of the century. The same story today could not have the same taboo-shattering impact. Nabokov was a moralist who had written a love story, a lyrical, funny, serious book, just as Woody is a moralist who made a lyrical, funny, serious film. The Mariel-Woody relationship was not perverse, but affectionate. There was no seduction or exploitation of an innocent young girl by an older man. The point was not that she was vulnerable, but that they were both vulnerable, and that she was a saner, wiser young woman than most of the neurotic "adults" in the movie.

# Present and future

The Film industry needs civilized entertainers. In mass entertainment at the present time, there are too few civilized voices to be heard amid the prevailing avalanche of vulgarity, philistinism and sensationalism, too few to represent understatement against overstatement, good taste against bad taste.

And, perhaps most important of all, language against imagery. What makes Woody Allen unique, perhaps, is not that he has made us laugh more consistently than anyone else, but that, almost alone, he has kept good talk on the screen. If literacy is the ability to speak and read and respond to language at levels of difficulty beyond "Far out!" and "really neat" and "Let's boogie!" then Woody is literate, and his current success is already a phenomenon of the popular arts.

In the effort to make quality movies, the question arises: how much substance can you give a character, or group of characters in a 90-minute comedy film? Answer: a lot, if the writing is good. The script needs to be succinct, not flabby. Brevity is not only the soul of wit, it is the essence of screenwriting. Actors can always be better than the lines you give them, but they can never be great without a good script. In 20 years Woody has developed and improved steadily, from monologue to dialogue, from one cartoon character to four or five real characters, from slapstick to sophisticated satire. The most important trend in his films is simply their improvement. Almost every time out, people have said "It's his best so far." *Manhattan* is his most relaxed film, has the best plot, the most convincing characterizations, and is funnier than anything he has done so far. Given his steady development it is no surprise to find that his latest is his best, but it is incredible that *Manhattan* is twice as good as any of his other films.

His stamina is to be admired, as is his strong stance on certain key topics. In the States today, more than ever, people who don't take drugs need a witty spokesman who is not scared of being thought square. As well as being consistently anti-drugs, Woody is anti-macho. The clarinet is not a phallic instrument. And, as we've seen, at a time when many directors have been content to let the visuals and sound effects do 90% of the work, he has been effectively verbal. *Manhattan* is his masterpiece partly because it is his most verbal film, the one which is most like a visualization of his brilliant night club routines.

Sight And Sound, an authoritative screen quaterly, has noted that his screen persona has become tougher through the Seventies. When menaced by a hood, Virgil Starkwell took off his own glasses and stomped on them, but Isaac Davis says that when Nazis march in New Jersey, satire is useless. What you need is bricks and baseball bats.

"In the past decade, between *Take The Money* and *Manhattan,* Woody Allen has smoothed and toughened his jumpy screen persona. The characters he has played (and with whom, to his dismay, he has become personally identified) have for one thing, moved up market: Fielding Mellish, in *Bananas,* was a product tester; Alan Felix in *Play It Again Sam,* a contributor to a movie magazine; Alvy Singer, in *Annie Hall,* an acclaimed comedian. Their enduring worries have slowly been tamed. Cowardice has given way to a sort of hesitant bravado. Women still cause complications; but where once the too-liberal application of after-shave lotion triggered uncontrollable pre-date jitters, we now find Isaac Davis tussling, as befits a man in his forties, with doubts about the meaning of work and the desirability of commitment."

His discipline is phenomenal, and seems to verge on masochism. Clearly, actors, writers and directors must expect to suffer in order to make a film. You have to be prepared to damage yourself, that's part of the game. To evolve a "perfect" scene or character, after days and days of rewriting and re-rehearsing, is to invest a lot of emotion in it. To give life to a character, then chop it up in an editing room, is painful. To cut a line or scene is to cut your own flesh. When the writer is also the director, and is on the screen as well, the choices are blurred and the anguish is multiplied.

Ralph Rosenblum reveals that Woody has long ago steeled himself to be objective about his work. "When a scene died, Woody never looked back," he says, admiringly. He was thrilled and surprised to meet a director who could be as ruthlessly realistic about weak or faltering material as an experienced editor like himself. "With so much of his material being removed, trimmed or modified in the editing, Woody's cool professionalism was an especially refreshing trait." He was helped by Woody's attitude which was "You have to subordinate everything to the laugh."

In time the *Interiors* chapter of Woody's career will not be seen as something important in itself but as a catalyst and turning point. Whatever one thinks of the movie, it clearly and strongly provides an invaluable stylistic link between *Annie Hall* and *Manhattan.* Each film is a chapter in an obvious progression: a colorful romp, followed by a pastel drama, followed by a black and white comedy classic.

*Annie Hall* is a jokey film, and *Manhattan* is a witty film. In between Woody got too severe and serious for his own good, had to come halfway back, and delivered his first masterpiece. Anyone shown all three films and told they were made in consecutive years could easily place them in order: *Annie Hall* in 1977, *Interiors* in 1978, and *Manhattan* in 1979. There is no way that he would have made *Annie Hall* after the other two, and no way that he knew enough to make *Manhattan* without the experience of having made *Interiors;* indeed, any director who had already made a mature comedy which was as satisfyingly serious as *Manhattan* might not even feel the need to attempt something as relentlessy somber as *Interiors.*

Where *Annie Hall* used color, cartoons, TV clips, flashbacks, slapstick, fantasy sequences and split screens, *Manhattan* is an exercise in minimalism: less is more. On at least one occasion both characters walk out of the frame, although we can still hear them talking. *Manhattan* was just black and white and Gershwin and craftsmanship, the skill that conceals skill. While the romping romance is fast on the eye, the mature comedy-drama is fast on the ear.

In America at the present time the two leading movie star - comedians are probably Richard Pryor and Woody Allen, two men who represent polar opposites. The wild and the mild, the visceral and the cerebral, the manic versus the depressive. Both confess, both are chroniclers and interpreters of our times, both articulate anxieties, and both draw heavily on their ethnic backgrounds. The differences between them are not only differences of a temperament, but of age and race. The older Jew is much more stable than the volatile young Black, who is prone to spontaneous explosions and egotistical excesses. The Jew is sane, while the Black crazy enough to put a bullet hole in the gold album which hangs on his bedroom wall, but not — we hope — crazy enough to become a victim of the hedonism and pharmacological abuses of the Rock Age Hollywood he so mercilessly satirizes.

Woody is unfashionably mild in a violent age. Other success stories of Seventies comedy have tended to be the products of more vulgar and aggressive sensibilities. Monty Python is often the humor of hate, full of psychopathic cruelties, although when it comes to violence in entertainment, the States still rules the world. Even in comedies about college life, barbarians like John Belushi are having food fights and riding motorbikes indoors.

*Being interviewed for Swedish TV by a double.*

*A fine head of hair.*

National Lampoon Editor-in-chief P.J. O'Rourke opines "What we do is oppressor comedy. Woody Allen says 'I'm just a regular schmuck like you'. Our kind of comedy says 'I'm OK, you're an asshole'. We are the ruling class. We are the insiders who have chosen to stand in the doorway and criticize the organization. Our comic pose is superior. It says 'I'm better than you and I'm going to destroy you.' It's an offensive, very aggressive form of humor."

Of course, cruelty in comedy has a long and illustrious history. Groucho

131

Marx is among the most heartless and opportunistic survivors ever seen on the screen. Audiences adored the blatant amorality of the Mae West persona, its mercenary ruthlessness as she chases playboy Cary Grant in *I'm No Angel.* Other heroes of cinematic comedy frequently revel in man's inhumanity to man. The philosophy of the comedy of cruelty is summed up in the title of a W.C. Fields film: *Never Give A Sucker An Even Break.* Billy Wilder is famed for his misanthropy.

Charlie Chaplin is typically a tramp trying to be a dandy. He clowns and charms but he can also be vicious. In *The Property Man* he makes a crippled old man carry a very heavy trunk, and beats him savagely, like a beast of burden. By contrast, Woody's humor is ceaselessly humane and mild-mannered. He is always Mr Nice Guy. Nowhere in any of his films is he as sadistic as Chaplin. As the prisoners line up for the firing squad in *Bananas,* they are not even tied, and when shot they slump forward but do not scream or bleed. He doesn't try to make it realistic, because it's a spoof, a send-up.

Offscreen Woody's behavior is nothing like the characters he plays in his films. He is a shy, sane, serious guy, not an awkward bumbler. He is never "on" in private, and will do almost anything to avoid a handshake. His long-time editor Ralph Rosenblum has seen Woody develop from a novice to one of the major forces in the film business. In 1968 he was ignorant, but in 1980 he is knowledgeable, a self-taught master of the medium who now has complete control of his movies, including hiring, casting and advertising.

"None of the popular accounts I've read," says Rosenblum, "come near to capturing the man I know — cerebral, cautious, judgmental, shrewd at covering his tracks, with a gentle but very mindful, even calculating, interpersonal style. He is smart, very smart, *frighteningly* smart."

"He has Prussian discipline. He's the only director I know who finishes a film and then, without any time off, without drinking or drugs or philandering, without celebration, gloating, or self-punishing regrets, goes quietly to work the following day on his next script. He practises his clarinet seven days a week. He finds time to write short stories for The New Yorker. He reads voluminously."

Rosenblum says Woody is an ascetic. "At times we spent hours earnestly hashing out problems... the tone of these conversations was easy and professional with surprisingly little kidding around, personal reflection or anything approaching intimacy. Woody is very private, very reserved, excruciatingly — at times maddeningly — controlled. He never snacks when

*Writer / Director / Actor*

he works; he never betrays what he's feeling. His paltry lunches, sometimes no more than a glass of club soda, are symbolic of his stoicism."

"In the ten years we've worked together, including the occasional times we've socialized, we've never shared a heartfelt concern, an uninhibited laugh, an open display of despair or anger. Neither of us is spontaneous about feelings, and Woody is one of the few people I know who is substantially less spontaneous than I."

It is surprising to read this in one of the most thoughtful, adult books about film ever written. Never? Not once in ten years? Extraordinary. Rosenblum also says: "I do not count Woody as a close friend, and yet we have so much in common I feel emotionally allied with him. We are both Jewish, both from Brooklyn, both perennially joyless, pessimistic about our chances for happiness, and easily sucked into low spirits."

With Woody, as with directors like Fellini and Truffaut who make autobiographical films to exorcise their obsessions, the question that has to be asked sooner or later is: How interesting are his obsessions? He has told the same type of jokes for fifteen years. By a roundabout route via San Marcos and gangsters and Russia, he has found a new, bigger market for those jokes. A successful New York comedian, given his first chance to direct, would be likely to make a New York comedy film, but Woody proved to be more adventurous than that. He went round in a circle, and came back home. His recent films have their own world, and their own world-view. As John Fordham noted in Time Out: "On his own admission, the characters he plays and the characters he writes inhabit a pretty narrow band of culture and temperament. (They tend to be neurotic media people, poets with cramp, devotees of psychoanalysis, modern art and Greenwich Village bookshops)."

We begin to wonder how many stories and insights can be gleaned from the affluent and arty circles where lesbians pop down to Barbados for weekends of sun and fun. Have we seen enough of their chic neuroses, adulteries, divorces, and custody battles? How many more good films can come out of all this?

My guess is, plenty.

New York is a goldmine. It is not a place, it is many places. It is not one state of mind, it is many states of mind. There are eight million stories in the Naked City and *Manhattan* is only one of them, *An Unmarried Woman* another, *Girlfriends* is a third and *Kramer vs Kramer* is a fourth. As a milieu for comic characters, situations and stories, it is inexhaustible, and still vastly under-exploited. It will yield a rich harvest for many years to

*Contemplating somebody else's navel*

come. There are scores of films there to be made, and it is just a question of who will bring them alive on the screen.

Woody Allen could lead the way. He now knows how to imagine and assemble a civilized entertainment which can reach a very large number of people and hold them for an hour and a half. As the king of this type of movie, he would be a fool to abdicate. No other individual has the reputation and the highly specific type of creative talents and connections to get into competition with him.

If you have finance and a good script, you can always get a film made. But if you have the money and a screenplay and you are chummy with Mariel Hemingway and Diane Keaton and you can ring up Meryl Streep and say "Can you give me five days?" then you have a huge advantage. These days, in this kind of modern urban comedy of relationships, if you have access to the Keaton/Streep/Marsha Mason caliber of actress you are halfway there, because these women are just so strong, so believable in what they do, that they can be relied on to give a fabulous performance which will carry half the film.

So far, Woody has under-exploited his milieu. In examining his career, that's the inevitable conclusion. His antics in diverse comedies have made us forget who he is. He has kept us so distracted in the last ten years by doing other things — talking to Bogart, having affairs with Diane Keaton, impersonating tuxedoed robots, being attacked by hairdryers, ordering wheelbarrows full of coleslaw, diving back and forward between 1812 and 2173 — that we have forgotten who he is, what he is, where he comes from and what he does best. In preferring fantasy to reportage, he has under-exploited his milieu.

If he wants to, he could go on and do for New York on film what Raymond Chandler did for Bay City, or what John Cheever and Updike have done for New England: to create and claim his own mythical territory, permanently. For all time. Because despite Woody's claims to the contrary, art is the way to beat death. The pursuit of immortality through art is not futile. Art is the only thing which remains after we are dead. Cinema became a major art form in the twentieth century, and Woody Allen has a chance now to become one of the major artists in his chosen medium of expression. The comedian who has gone on and on and on about being afraid of Death will probably peg out peacefully in his sleep at the age of 106, secure in the knowledge that Isaac and Alvy and all his other alter-egos will be walking and joking their way across the screens of the world for decades to come.

So far, Woody has shown himself to be a romantic, a moralist, and a self-educated, self-motivated artist. How great he is, it's far too soon to say. All we know is that talent does what it can, and genius does what it must, and as John Updike remarked in his review of Franny And Zooey "the willingness to risk excess on behalf of one's obsessions is what distinguishes artists from entertainers, and what makes some artists adventurers on behalf of us all."

Ten years in, he is still a young director. Blake Edwards is still directing hit films at 58. Billy Wilder made *Fedora* when he was 70. John Huston is making a thriller called *Phobia* at the age of 74, Otto Preminger is 75, and Hitchcock was still directing at 81. At the tender age of 44, Woody Allen is still a young whippersnapper. Remember, Robert Altman was already 45 when he directed M*A*S*H in 1970.

Woody is now handily placed to become one of the truly great American film directors. His future activities depend on how much he wants to stay on the screen. He did *Play It Again, Sam* in which he was 29 and his wife had left him, and he did *Manhattan* in which he is 42 and both his wives have left him. His progression is not one of subject matter, but of confidence and craftsmanship, and he must know that having already done plenty in front of the camera the real challenge for the future is in writing and directing. The big step for Woody is probably not his debut as a director of serious drama, but the serious comedy film which he only writes and directs. He can make bolder and better films, and possibly be more prolific, but probably not while he is acting in his own vehicles. It's just a question of whether he wants to get off the screen, and whether he can stand to see someone else up there getting the laughs for something he has written.

Whatever the future holds, America needs New York, and New York needs Woody Allen, and that Woody should stay home more. There is no place like home, because home is where you hang your hat and your neuroses and your clarinet. And as the 1980s start, the nice New Yorker is one of the few people who can be trusted to do something decent amidst all the junk.

# Filmography

**WHATS NEW PUSSYCAT    1965**

*Producer:*      Charles K. Feldman

*Director:*      Clive Donner

*Main Actors:*   Peter Sellers: Fritz Fassbender
                Peter O'Toole: Michael James
                Romy Schneider: Card Werner
                Capucine: Renee Lefebvre
                Paula Prentiss: Liz
                Woody Allen: Victor Shakapopolis

*(Guest Star)*   Ursula Andress: Rita

**CASINO ROYALE    1965**

*Producer:*      Charles K. Feldman (x Jerry Bresler)

*Director:*      John Huston, Ken Hughes, Val Guest, Robert Parrish, Joe McGrath
Shepperton Studios

*Main Actors:*   Peter Sellers: Evelyn Tremble (J. B. 007)
                Ursula Andress: Vesper Lynd (007)
                Orson Welles: Le Chiffre
                David Niven: Sir James Bond
                Joanna Pettet: Mata Bond
                Daliah Lavi: The Detainer (007)
                Deborah Kerr: Agent Mimi (Alias Lady Fiona)
                Woody Allen: Jimmy Bond (Dr. Noah)

## WHATS UP TIGER LILLY    1966
Japanese (dubbed by W.A. screenplay)
film


## THE FRONT    1969
*Producer and Director:* Martin Ritt

*Main Actors:*    Woody Allen: Howard Prince
Zero Mostel: Hecky Brown
Herschel Bernadi: Phil Sussman
Michael Murphy: Alfred Miller
Andrea Marcovicci: Florence Barrett
Remak Ramsay: Henessey
Marvin Lichterman: Myer Prince


## TAKE THE MONEY AND RUN    1969
*Producer:*    Charles H. Joffe    shums of Baltimore

*Director:*    Woody Allen

*Main Actors:*    Woody Allen: Virgil Starkwell
Jane Margolin: Louise
Jacquelyn Hyde: Miss Blair
Marcel Hillaire: Fritz
Lonny Chapman: Jake
Jan Merlin: Al
James Anderson: Chain Gang Warden
Howard Storm: Fred


## BANANAS    1971
*Producer:*    Jack Grossberg

*Director:*    Woody Allen

Filmed on locations in Puerto Rico and New York

*Main Actors:*    Woody Allen: Fielding Mellish
Louise Lasser: Nancy
Carlos Montalban: General Emilio M. Vargus
Natividad Abascal: Yolanda
Jacobo Morales: Esposito
Miguel Suarez: Luis
David Ortiz: Sanchez


## EVERYTHING YOU ALWAYS WANTED TO KNOW ABOUT SEX... ASK
*Producer:*    Charles H. Joffe

*Director:*    Woody Allen

*Main Actors:*    Woody Allen: Victor/Fabrizio/The Fool/Sperm
John Carradine: Doctor Bernado

Lon Jacobi: Sam
Louise Lasser: Gina
Anthony Quayle: The King
Tony Randall: The Operator
Lynn Redgrave: The Queen
Burt Reynolds: Switchboard
Gene Wilder: Dr. Ross


## PLAY IT AGAIN SAM   1972
*Producer:*     Arthur P. Jacobs

*Director:*     Herbert Ross

*Main Actors:*  Woody Allen: Alan
Diane Keaton: Linda
Tony Roberts: Dick
Jerry Lacy: Bogart
Susan Anspach: Nancy
Jennifer Salt: Sharon
Joy Bang: Julie


## SLEEPER   1974
*Producer:*     Jack Crossberg

*Director:*     Woody Allen

*Main Actors:*  Woody Allen: Miles Monroe
Diane Keaton: Linda Schlesser
John Beck: Erno Windt
Mary Gregory: Dr. Melik
Don Keefer: Dr. Tryon
Don McLiam: Dr. Argon
Bartlett Robinson: Dr. Orva
Chris Forbes: Rainer Krebs


## LOVE AND DEATH   1975
*Producer:*     Charles H. Joffe

*Director:*     Woody Allen

Filming: Budapest, Hungary, Paris

*Main Actors:*  Woody Allen: Boris
Diane Keaton: Sonja
Lloyd Battista: Don Francisco
Olga Georges-Picot: Countess Alexandrovna
Alfred Lutter II: Boris
Norman Rose: Death
James Tolkan: Napoleon
Howard Vernon: General Leveque

## ANNIE HALL   1977

*Producer:*    Charles H. Joffe

*Director:*    Woody Allen

Filmed few scenes Pathe Studios 106th St. and Park Av. also N.Y. City, L.A.; Manhattan

*Main Actors:*   Woody Allen: Alvy Singer
Diane Keaton: Annie Hall
Tony Roberts: Rob
Carl Kane: Alison
Paul Simon: Tony Lacey
Janet Margolin: Robin
Coileen Dewhurst: Mom Hall

## INTERIORS   1978

*Producer:*    Charles H. Joffe

*Director:*    Woody Allen

*Main Actors:*   Kristin Griffith: Flyn
Marybeth Hunt: Joey
Richard Jordan: Frederick
Diane Keaton: Renata
E.G. Marshall: Arthur
Geraldine Page: Eve
Sam Waterston: Mike

## MANHATTAN   1979

*Producer:*    Charles H. Joffe

*Director:*    Woody Allen

*Main Actors:*   Woody Allen: Isaac Davis
Diane Keaton: Mary Wilke
Michael Murphy: Yale
Mariel Hemingway: Tracy
Meryl Streep: Jill
Anne Byrne: Emily
Karen Ludwig: Connie
Michael O'Donoghne: Dennis